THE SPIRIT OF CHRISTMAS
COOKBOOK
Volume 4

The holidays are a time for enjoying the company of family and friends, and the best conversations take place over plates full of scrumptious foods. Our new volume in The Spirit of Christmas Cookbook *series is a valuable resource for all kinds of holiday cooking, from munchies to multi-course meals. We've selected recipes for great starts, like spicy peppered cheese biscuits and low-fat salmon pâté, and decadent desserts such as chocolate-covered-cherry pie and maple-pecan cookies. For the main course you'll find an incredible glazed roast turkey with horseradish sauce, fresh ham covered in a tart and tangy cranberry glaze, and more! Our collection of more than 240 recipes will make sure you're prepared for an open house, a family gathering, or drop-in guests. So keep the goodies coming, no matter what style of celebrating you prefer, and bask in the warm glow of a tasty Christmas!*

LEISURE ARTS, INC.
Little Rock, Arkansas

THE SPIRIT OF CHRISTMAS
COOKBOOK
Volume 4

EDITORIAL STAFF

Vice President and Editor-in-Chief: Anne Van Wagner Childs
Executive Director: Sandra Graham Case
Test Kitchen Director/Foods Editor: Celia Fahr Harkey, R.D.
Editorial Director: Susan Frantz Wiles
Creative Art Director: Gloria Bearden

FOODS
Assistant Foods Editor: Jane Kenner Prather
Food Copy Editor: Judy Millard
Test Kitchen Home Economist: Rose Glass Klein
Test Kitchen Coordinator: Nora Faye Taylor
Test Kitchen Assistants: Brandy Black Alewine,
    Camille T. Alstadt, and Donna Huffner Spencer

EDITORIAL
Managing Editor: Linda L. Trimble
Associate Editors: Darla Burdette Kelsay,
    Stacey Robertson Marshall, and Janice Teipen Wojcik
Copy Editor: Terri Leming Davidson

ART
Book/Magazine Graphics Art Director: Diane Thomas
Production Artist: Linda Chambers
Color Technician: Mark Hawkins
Photography Stylist: Karen Smart Hall
Publishing Systems Administrator: Cindy Lumpkin
Publishing Systems Assistant: Myra Means

PROMOTIONS
Managing Editor: Alan Caudle
Associate Editor: Steven M. Cooper
Designer: Dale Rowett
Art Director: Linda Lovette Smart

BUSINESS STAFF

Publisher: Rick Barton
Vice President and General Manager: Thomas L. Carlisle
Vice President, Finance: Tom Siebenmorgen
Vice President, Retail Marketing: Bob Humphrey
Vice President, National Accounts: Pam Stebbins

Retail Marketing Director: Margaret Sweetin
General Merchandise Manager: Cathy Laird
Distribution Director: Rob Thieme
Retail Customer Service Manager: Wanda Price
Print Production Manager: Fred F. Pruss

We would like to extend our thanks to Christy Kalder, Micah McConnell, Susan Warren Reeves, R.D., and Kay Wright for their contributions as former foods editors and consultants for *The Spirit of Christmas* and *Memories in the Making* volumes from which we chose our recipes.

Library of Congress Catalog Card Number 97-73650
International Standard Book Number 1-57486-138-7

10 9 8 7 6 5 4 3 2 1

TABLE OF CONTENTS

TABLE OF CONTENTS
(Continued)

TABLE OF CONTENTS
(Continued)

SANTA'S SWEETSHOP

Cookies and candies and cupcakes, oh my! Our array of scrumptious treats would satisfy even Santa's sweet tooth. You'll find delightfully rich candy bars, fabulous fudge, and delicately glazed cookies — and they're all perfect for adding a delicious finish to your holiday gatherings. So open your door and welcome one and all with the tasty tidbits in this magnificent collection.

Crispy-Crunchy Candy Bars (recipe on page 8) feature a yummy filling of vanilla frosting and candy-coated chocolates sandwiched between two layers of marshmallow cereal squares.

CRISPY-CRUNCHY CANDY BARS (Shown on pages 6 and 7)

2 1/2 cups red and green candy-
      coated mini chocolate pieces
1 can (16 ounces) vanilla-flavored
      ready-to-spread frosting
1/2 cup butter or margarine, divided
10 cups miniature marshmallows,
      divided
1 cup creamy peanut butter,
      divided
1/2 cup light corn syrup, divided
10 cups crispy rice cereal, divided

In a small bowl, stir together chocolate pieces and frosting; set aside. Microwave 1/4 cup butter in a large microwave-safe bowl until butter melts. Stir in 5 cups marshmallows and microwave on high power (100%) about 1 minute or until marshmallows begin to soften; stir until marshmallows melt. Add 1/2 cup peanut butter and 1/4 cup corn syrup. Stir in 5 cups cereal until well blended. With greased hands, press half of cereal mixture into each of 2 greased 7 x 11-inch baking dishes. Spread each cereal layer with frosting mixture. Make a second batch of cereal mixture using remaining butter, marshmallows, peanut butter, corn syrup, and cereal. Carefully press second batch of cereal mixture over frosting layer in each pan. Cover and chill 30 minutes or until mixture is firm. Cut into 2-inch squares. Store in an airtight container.
Yield: about 15 bars in each baking dish

SNOWFLAKE MERINGUE COOKIES

4 egg whites
1 1/2 cups confectioners sugar
1 teaspoon almond extract
1/2 teaspoon ground cinnamon
1/2 teaspoon cream of tartar
      White coarse decorating sugar

Trace pattern onto tracing paper. Cover baking sheets with waxed paper. In a large bowl, beat egg whites until foamy. Add confectioners sugar, almond extract, cinnamon, and cream of tartar; beat until very stiff. Spoon meringue into a pastry bag fitted with a small star tip. For each cookie, place pattern under waxed paper and use as a guide to pipe meringue onto waxed paper. Sprinkle with decorating sugar. Allow cookies to sit at room temperature 30 minutes.

Preheat oven to 200 degrees. Bake 2 hours. Leaving warm cookies on waxed paper, transfer to a smooth surface; cool completely. Carefully peel away waxed paper. Store in an airtight container.
Yield: about 2 1/2 dozen cookies

SEAFOAM DIVINITY

2 1/2 cups firmly packed brown sugar
1/2 cup water
1/4 cup dark corn syrup
2 teaspoons white vinegar
2 egg whites
1 teaspoon vanilla extract
1 cup finely chopped pecans
      Pecan halves to garnish

Butter sides of a heavy medium saucepan. Combine brown sugar, water, corn syrup, and vinegar in saucepan. Stirring constantly, cook over medium heat until sugar dissolves. Using a pastry brush dipped in hot water, wash down any sugar crystals on sides of pan. Attach a candy thermometer to pan, making sure thermometer does not touch bottom of pan. Increase heat to medium high and bring to a boil. While mixture is boiling, use highest speed of an electric mixer to beat egg whites in a large bowl until stiff; set aside. Cook mixture, without stirring, until it reaches hard-ball stage (approximately 250 to 268 degrees). Test about 1/2 teaspoon mixture in ice water. Mixture will roll into a hard ball in ice water and will remain hard when removed from water. Remove from heat. Beating at low speed, slowly pour hot mixture into egg whites. Add vanilla and increase speed of mixer to high. Continue to beat 2 1/2 to 3 1/2 minutes or just until mixture holds its shape. Quickly stir in chopped pecans; drop heaping teaspoonfuls of candy onto greased aluminum foil. Press a pecan half into center of each candy. Allow candy to harden. Store in an airtight container.
Yield: about 3 1/2 dozen candies

Light and delicate, Snowflake Meringue Cookies are flavored with almond extract and cinnamon and piped into a snowflake pattern using a pastry bag.

ORANGE JELLY CANDIES

- 3/4 cup apple juice
- 2 packages (1 3/4 ounces each) powdered fruit pectin
- 1/2 teaspoon baking soda
- 1 cup sugar
- 1 cup light corn syrup
- 1/2 teaspoon orange extract
  Orange paste food coloring
  Sugar

Line an 8-inch square baking pan with aluminum foil, extending foil over 2 sides of pan; grease foil. In a small saucepan, combine apple juice and fruit pectin. Stir in baking soda (mixture will foam). In a heavy medium saucepan, combine 1 cup sugar and corn syrup. Whisking pectin mixture constantly and stirring sugar mixture constantly, cook both mixtures at the same time over medium-high heat about 5 minutes or until pectin mixture dissolves and sugar mixture comes to a rolling boil. Continuing to stir, slowly pour pectin mixture into sugar mixture. Stirring constantly, continue to boil 4 minutes. Remove from heat and stir in orange extract; tint orange. Pour into prepared pan. Chill about 30 minutes or until firm enough to cut.

Use ends of foil to lift candy from pan. Use a wet 1-inch aspic cutter to cut candy into desired shapes. Roll candies in sugar. Store in a single layer in an airtight container in refrigerator.
Yield: about 5 dozen candies

Made with brown sugar, Seafoam Divinity (left) is a yummy confection that's sure to satisfy the sweetest sweet tooth. Packed with citrus flavor, Orange Jelly Candies can be cut in fun shapes and rolled in sugar for an enchanting finish.

MACADAMIA NUT CANDIED CORN

24 cups popped popcorn
2 cups macadamia nuts
1³/₄ cups sugar
1 cup butter or margarine
¹/₂ cup light corn syrup
¹/₂ teaspoon salt
3 cups miniature marshmallows
¹/₄ teaspoon butter flavoring

Preheat oven to 250 degrees. Place popcorn and macadamia nuts in a greased large roasting pan. In a heavy large saucepan, combine sugar, butter, corn syrup, and salt over medium heat. Stirring constantly, bring to a boil. Boil 2 minutes without stirring. Remove from heat. Add marshmallows; stir until melted. Stir in butter flavoring. Pour marshmallow mixture over popcorn mixture; stir until well coated. Bake 1 hour, stirring every 15 minutes. Spread on lightly greased aluminum foil to cool. Store in an airtight container.
Yield: about 26 cups candied corn

GERMAN CHOCOLATE FUDGE

4 packages (4 ounces each) German baking chocolate, chopped
1 can (14 ounces) sweetened condensed milk
1 cup chopped pecans, toasted
1 cup flaked coconut
2 teaspoons vanilla extract

Line an 8-inch square baking pan with aluminum foil, extending foil over 2 sides of pan; grease foil. Combine chocolate and sweetened condensed milk in a large microwave-safe bowl. Microwave until chocolate softens; stir mixture until chocolate melts. Stir in pecans, coconut, and vanilla. Spread mixture into prepared pan. Cover and chill 2 hours or until firm.

Use ends of foil to lift fudge from pan. Cut into 1-inch squares. Store in an airtight container in a cool place.
Yield: about 4 dozen pieces fudge

Macadamia Nut Candied Corn is a crunchy gourmet treat that's perfect for satisfying the munchies. Laden with toasted pecans and coconut, German Chocolate Fudge is a rich, dark confection friends will savor.

GINGERBREAD COOKIES IN A GINGERBREAD BOWL

1 cup butter or margarine, softened
3/4 cup firmly packed brown sugar
1/2 cup granulated sugar
1/3 cup light molasses
3/4 cup dark corn syrup
3 eggs
8 1/2 cups all-purpose flour
1 tablespoon baking soda
1 teaspoon salt
1 teaspoon **each** ground ginger, ground cloves, ground cinnamon, and ground allspice

In a large bowl, cream butter and sugars until fluffy. Beat in molasses, corn syrup, and eggs until smooth. In another large bowl, combine flour, baking soda, salt, and spices. Add dry ingredients to creamed mixture; stir until well combined (dough will be stiff). Divide dough into fourths. Wrap in plastic wrap and chill 2 hours or until well chilled.

Preheat oven to 350 degrees. Smoothly cover the outside of a 1-quart ovenproof glass bowl with aluminum foil; grease foil. On a lightly floured surface, use a floured rolling pin to roll out one fourth of dough into a 1/4-inch-thick circle. Transfer dough to outside of foil-lined bowl, pressing dough firmly onto bowl. Use a 1-inch-wide heart-shaped cookie cutter to cut out hearts around bowl. Place inverted bowl on an ungreased baking sheet and bake 25 to 30 minutes or until dough is lightly browned and firm to the touch. Allow to cool on bowl. Carefully loosen foil; remove foil and gingerbread bowl from glass bowl. Remove foil from gingerbread bowl.

Roll out remaining dough to 1/8-inch thickness. Cut out cookies using desired cookie cutters. Place on a lightly greased baking sheet. Bake 8 to 10 minutes or until lightly browned. Transfer to a wire rack to cool. Store cookies in an airtight container.
Yield: 1 bowl and about 3 dozen cookies

Lightly spiced Gingerbread Cookies fill an edible Gingerbread Bowl made from the same recipe. These festive cookies are cut in house, heart, and pineapple shapes — traditional symbols of hospitality.

Two chocolaty treats, Chocolate Chip-Mocha Bars have a rich coffee flavor, and Chocolate-Pecan Cookies are chock-full of nuts.

CHOCOLATE CHIP-MOCHA BARS

- 2 tablespoons instant coffee granules
- 2 tablespoons hot water
- 1 package (18¼ ounces) yellow cake mix
- 1 cup firmly packed brown sugar
- ½ cup butter or margarine, softened
- 2 eggs
- 2 teaspoons vanilla extract
- 3 cups (one 12-ounce and one 6-ounce package) semisweet chocolate chips, divided

Preheat oven to 350 degrees. In a large bowl, combine coffee granules and water. Add cake mix, brown sugar, butter, eggs, and vanilla to coffee mixture; beat until smooth. Stir in 2 cups chocolate chips. Spoon batter into a greased 9 x 13-inch baking pan. Bake 40 to 45 minutes or until edges begin to pull away from sides of pan. Cool completely in pan.

Cut into 1 x 2-inch bars. Place remaining 1 cup chocolate chips in a disposable pastry bag. Microwave on medium power (50%) at 30 second intervals until chocolate melts. Cut the end of the bag to make a small hole. Drizzle chocolate over bars. Allow chocolate to harden. Store in an airtight container.
Yield: about 3 dozen bars

CHOCOLATE-PECAN COOKIES

- ¾ cup butter or margarine, softened
- 1 cup firmly packed brown sugar
- 1 egg yolk
- 1 teaspoon vanilla extract
- 1½ cups all-purpose flour
- ⅓ cup cocoa
- 1 cup finely chopped pecans
  Pecan halves

Preheat oven to 350 degrees. In a medium bowl, cream butter and brown sugar. Beat in egg yolk and vanilla. In a small bowl, combine flour and cocoa. Add dry ingredients to creamed mixture; stir until a soft dough forms. Stir in chopped pecans. Drop heaping teaspoonfuls of dough 1 inch apart onto a greased baking sheet. Press 1 pecan half into each cookie. Bake 8 to 10 minutes or until firm. Transfer to a wire rack to cool completely. Store in an airtight container.
Yield: about 5 dozen cookies

CARAMELIZED FRUIT CLUSTERS

- 1 cup chopped candied red cherries
- 1 cup chopped candied green cherries
- 1 cup chopped candied pineapple
- 1 cup chopped pecans
- 2 cups sugar
- 1 cup water
- 1 teaspoon white vinegar
- 1 teaspoon vanilla extract

In a medium bowl, combine candied fruit and pecans. Loosely spoon a heaping tablespoonful of fruit mixture into each greased cup of a miniature muffin pan (do not press fruit into cup). Combine sugar, water, vinegar, and vanilla in a heavy medium skillet. Swirling pan occasionally, cook sugar mixture about 25 to 30 minutes over medium heat or until sugar has caramelized and is golden brown in color. Remove mixture from heat. Carefully and quickly spoon hot syrup over fruit mixture in each muffin cup until fruit is almost covered. (If sugar mixture begins to harden in skillet, return to low heat.) Allow candies to harden; transfer to paper candy cups. Store in a single layer in an airtight container in refrigerator.
Yield: about 3 dozen candies

To create our luscious Caramelized Fruit Clusters, chopped pecans and candied cherry and pineapple "jewels" are drenched in a golden syrup.

Toasted Pecan Nougat is a sweet, chewy confection that will bring folks back for more. Each square is packed with crunchy chopped nuts.

TOASTED PECAN NOUGAT

Use a heavy-duty mixer to make this candy.

    1   tablespoon plus 1 teaspoon
          cornstarch, divided
 1 1/2 cups sugar
    1   cup light corn syrup
  1/2   cup water
  1/8   teaspoon salt
    2   egg whites
  1/8   teaspoon cream of tartar
    1   teaspoon vanilla extract
    1   teaspoon almond extract
    1   cup chopped pecans, toasted

Line a 9-inch square baking pan with aluminum foil, extending foil over 2 sides of pan. Grease foil and sprinkle with 1 teaspoon cornstarch. In a heavy large saucepan, combine sugar and remaining 1 tablespoon cornstarch; stir in corn syrup, water, and salt. Stirring constantly, cook over medium-low heat until sugar dissolves. Using a pastry brush dipped in hot water, wash down any sugar crystals on sides of pan. Attach a candy thermometer to pan, making sure thermometer does not touch bottom of pan. Increase heat to medium and bring to a boil. While mixture is boiling, beat egg whites and cream of tartar in a medium bowl until stiff; set aside. Cook sugar mixture, without stirring, until mixture reaches 286 degrees. While beating at high speed, slowly pour hot mixture over egg white mixture. Beat in extracts. Continue to beat until candy begins to hold its shape and lose its gloss. Stir in pecans. Press mixture into prepared pan. Use a wet knife to score warm nougat into 1-inch squares. Allow to cool.

Use ends of foil to lift nougat from pan. Use a serrated knife and a sawing motion to cut into squares. Place each nougat piece in a candy cup and store in an airtight container in refrigerator.

Yield: about 6 dozen pieces nougat

CHOCOLATE-DIPPED FRUIT AND NUT CANDIES

  3/4 cup chopped dried apricots
  3/4 cup chopped dates
  3/4 cup chopped walnuts
  1/2 cup flaked coconut
  1/4 cup butter or margarine, softened
  1/4 cup light corn syrup
  1/2 teaspoon vanilla extract
    3 cups confectioners sugar
    8 ounces chocolate candy coating,
          chopped
    4 ounces semisweet baking
          chocolate, chopped

Process apricots, dates, walnuts, and coconut in a food processor until coarsely chopped. In a medium bowl, cream butter and corn syrup until fluffy. Stir in vanilla. Beating with an electric mixer, gradually add confectioners sugar to butter mixture until too stiff to beat. Stir in remaining sugar. Pour mixture onto a dampened smooth surface. Knead until very smooth and creamy. Knead in fruit mixture. Shape rounded teaspoonfuls of candy into balls. Place on waxed paper. Loosely cover with waxed paper and allow to dry overnight at room temperature.

Stirring frequently, melt candy coating and baking chocolate in a heavy small saucepan over low heat. Remove from heat (if chocolate mixture begins to harden, return to heat). Dip each candy into chocolate. Place on a baking sheet lined with waxed paper. Dip fork into remaining chocolate; swirl over candies. Chill until firm. Store in an airtight container in a cool place.

Yield: about 4 1/2 dozen candies

Chocolate-Dipped Fruit and Nut Candies and Cranberry-Orange Fudge are two luscious goodies that connoisseurs of confections will love!

CRANBERRY-ORANGE FUDGE

1 cup sweetened dried cranberries
2 tablespoons orange juice
2 cups sugar
1 cup whipping cream
1 tablespoon light corn syrup
2 tablespoons butter or margarine
1 teaspoon vanilla extract
1/2 cup finely chopped candied orange peel

Combine cranberries and orange juice in a small microwave-safe bowl. Cover and microwave on high power (100%) 2 minutes, stirring after 1 minute. Allow covered cranberry mixture to stand 10 minutes. Pulse process mixture in a food processor until coarsely chopped.

Line an 8-inch square baking pan with aluminum foil, extending foil over 2 sides of pan; grease foil. Butter sides of a heavy large saucepan. Combine sugar, whipping cream, and corn syrup in saucepan. Stirring constantly, cook over medium-low heat until sugar dissolves. Using a pastry brush dipped in hot water, wash down any sugar crystals on sides of pan. Attach a candy thermometer to pan, making sure thermometer does not touch bottom of pan. Increase heat to medium and bring to a boil. Cook, without stirring, until mixture reaches soft-ball stage (approximately 234 to 240 degrees). Test about 1/2 teaspoon mixture in ice

water. Mixture will easily form a ball in ice water but will flatten when removed from water. Place saucepan in 2 inches of cold water in sink. Add butter and vanilla; do not stir. Cool to approximately 110 degrees. Remove from sink. Using medium speed of an electric mixer, beat until fudge thickens and begins to lose its gloss. Stir in orange peel and cranberries. Pour into prepared pan. Cover and chill 2 hours or until firm.

Use ends of foil to lift fudge from pan. Cut into 1-inch squares, wiping knife clean between cuts. Store in an airtight container in refrigerator.
Yield: about 4 dozen pieces fudge

ORANGE CREAMS

2 cups sugar
¼ cup light corn syrup
¾ cup milk
⅛ teaspoon salt
  Zest and juice from 1 medium
    orange
¼ cup butter
1 teaspoon vanilla extract
1½ cups chopped pecans, lightly
    toasted

Butter sides of a heavy medium saucepan. Combine sugar, corn syrup, milk, and salt in pan. Stirring constantly, cook over medium-low heat until sugar dissolves. Using a pastry brush dipped in hot water, wash down any sugar crystals on sides of pan. Attach a candy thermometer to pan, making sure thermometer does not touch bottom of pan. Increase heat to medium and bring to a boil. Stir in orange juice. Cook, without stirring, until mixture reaches soft-ball stage (234 to 240 degrees). Test abut ½ teaspoon mixture in ice water. Mixture will easily form a ball in ice water but will flatten when removed from water. Add orange zest and cook 1 minute longer. Remove from heat. Cool to about 110 degrees. Stir in butter and vanilla. Using medium speed of an electric mixer, beat until candy thickens and begins to lose its gloss. Stir in pecans. Drop by teaspoonfuls onto waxed paper. Let candy harden. Store in an airtight container.
Yield: about 3 dozen pieces

CHOCOLATE CHIPS

These chips are best if eaten or shared with friends soon after preparing.

6 ounces chocolate candy coating,
    chopped
24 ridge-style potato chips

Melt candy coating in top of a double boiler over hot, not simmering, water. Carefully dip half of each potato chip into coating. Place on waxed paper to let coating harden. Serve immediately.
Yield: 24 chips

CHOCOLATE-APRICOT ROLLS

16 large marshmallows, cut into
    pieces
2 tablespoons milk
4 ounces chocolate candy
    coating, melted
1 cup finely chopped pecans
1 cup chopped dried apricots

Combine marshmallows and milk in top of a double boiler; stir until marshmallows melt. Remove from heat. Stir in melted candy coating, pecans, and apricots. With greased hands, shape mixture into two 6-inch-long rolls. Wrap in plastic wrap and chill until firm. Cut into ¼-inch slices.
Yield: about 4 dozen pieces

A tasty combination of sweet and salty, Chocolate Chips are made by dipping potato chips in melted candy coating. Fresh orange and toasted pecans make Orange Creams an appealing treat. Delicious Chocolate-Apricot Rolls are a quick-and-easy, no-fuss candy.

Creamy Peanut Butter Fudge will be a welcome treat any time. For a nutty twist, try dipping the candy in chocolate and pecans!

PEANUT BUTTER FUDGE

1   cup granulated sugar
1   cup firmly packed brown sugar
1   cup evaporated milk
1/4   cup light corn syrup
1/8   teaspoon salt
1   cup large marshmallows, cut
      into pieces
1/2   cup smooth peanut butter
2   tablespoons butter
1   teaspoon vanilla extract

Butter sides of a medium saucepan. Combine sugars, milk, corn syrup, and salt in pan. Stirring constantly, cook over medium-low heat until sugar dissolves. Using a pastry brush dipped in hot water, wash down any sugar crystals on sides of pan. Attach a candy thermometer to pan, making sure thermometer does not touch bottom of pan. Increase heat to medium and bring to a boil. Cook, without stirring, until mixture reaches soft-ball stage (234 to 240 degrees). Test about 1/2 teaspoon mixture in ice water. Mixture will easily form a ball in ice water but will flatten when removed from water. Add marshmallows, peanut butter, and butter; stir until smooth. Stir in vanilla. Using medium speed of an electric mixer, beat until fudge thickens and begins to lose its gloss. Pour into a buttered 8-inch square pan. Cool completely. Cut fudge into 1 1/2-inch squares, then cut in half diagonally to form triangles. Store in an airtight container or see Chocolate-Dipped Variation.

Yield: 1 pound, 10 ounces fudge or about 50 triangles

CHOCOLATE-DIPPED VARIATION

3   ounces chocolate candy
      coating, melted
1/2   cup chopped pecans, finely
      ground

Using half of fudge pieces, dip edges into melted chocolate, then into pecans. Place on waxed paper to let chocolate harden. Store in an airtight container.

17

Lightly sweetened with brown sugar, Cashew Cookies get their mild, nutty flavor from chopped cashews and cream cheese.

GINGER BEARS

- 2 cups all-purpose flour
- 1/3 cup sugar
- 1 teaspoon ground cinnamon
- 1 teaspoon ground ginger
- 1 teaspoon baking powder
- 1/4 teaspoon baking soda
- 1/2 cup butter or margarine
- 1/2 cup molasses
- 2 tablespoons hot water
- 1/2 cup strawberry preserves
  Purchased brown decorating icing
  Red candy-coated chocolate pieces

Trace pattern onto stencil plastic; cut out. Sift flour, sugar, cinnamon, ginger, baking powder, and baking soda into a large bowl. In a small saucepan, melt butter over low heat. Stir in molasses. Stir butter mixture and water into dry ingredients; knead until a soft dough forms. Cover and chill 1 hour.

Preheat oven to 375 degrees. On a lightly floured surface, use a floured rolling pin to roll out dough to 1/8-inch thickness. Use pattern and a sharp knife to cut out an even number of cookies. Place half of cookies on greased baking sheets. Spoon about 1 teaspoon preserves in center of each cookie. Top with remaining cookies and crimp edges with a fork. Bake 10 to 12 minutes or until edges are lightly browned. Cool completely on a wire rack.

Use a small round tip to pipe icing for eyes and mouth on each cookie. Use a small amount of icing to secure a candy-coated piece on each cookie for nose. Allow icing to harden. Store in an airtight container.
Yield: about 2 dozen cookies

CASHEW COOKIES

- 1/2 cup butter or margarine, softened
- 3/4 cup firmly packed brown sugar
- 4 ounces cream cheese, softened
- 1 egg
- 2 tablespoons milk
- 1 teaspoon vanilla extract
- 2 cups all-purpose flour
- 3/4 teaspoon baking powder
- 3/4 teaspoon baking soda
- 1/4 teaspoon salt
- 1 1/2 cups chopped lightly salted cashews

Preheat oven to 350 degrees. In a large bowl, cream butter, brown sugar, and cream cheese until fluffy. Add egg, milk, and vanilla; beat until smooth. Sift flour, baking powder, baking soda, and salt into a small bowl. Add dry ingredients to creamed mixture; stir until a soft dough forms. Stir in cashews. Shape dough into 1-inch balls. Place on a greased baking sheet. Bake 10 to 12 minutes or until lightly browned. Transfer cookies to a wire rack to cool. Store in an airtight container.
Yield: about 5 dozen cookies

For a fruity surprise, Ginger Bears have a spoonful of strawberry preserves baked in the center of each spicy cookie.

Heavenly Caramelized Cake Squares are candy-like morsels created by dipping bits of light, fluffy angel food cake into freshly made caramel, then rolling them in nuts.

CARAMELIZED CAKE SQUARES

    2   cups butter or margarine
    2   cups firmly packed brown sugar
    1   purchased (7-inch diameter)
          angel food cake, cut into
          1-inch cubes
    4   cups finely chopped pecans

In a large saucepan, combine butter and brown sugar over medium heat. Stirring constantly, cook until sugar dissolves. Increase heat to medium high and bring to a boil. Cook until mixture reaches soft-ball stage (234 to 240 degrees); remove from heat. Using tongs, dip cake cubes in mixture; roll in pecans. Place on waxed paper to cool completely. Store in an airtight container.
Yield: about 5 dozen cake squares

CHOCOLATE SHORTBREAD

    1   cup butter, softened
  2/3   cup confectioners sugar
    1   teaspoon vanilla extract
 1 1/2 cups all-purpose flour
  1/4   cup cocoa
  1/4   teaspoon salt
        Confectioners sugar

In a large bowl, cream butter, confectioners sugar, and vanilla until fluffy. In a small bowl, combine flour, cocoa, and salt. Add flour mixture to creamed mixture; stir until well blended. Wrap dough in plastic wrap and chill 30 minutes.

Preheat oven to 300 degrees. Press dough into a 10 1/2 x 15 1/2-inch jellyroll pan. Bake 30 minutes. Remove from oven and use a 2-inch-wide heart-shaped cookie cutter to cut out warm shortbread. Transfer cookies to a wire rack with waxed paper underneath to cool. Sift confectioners sugar over cooled cookies. Store in an airtight container.
Yield: about 2 dozen cookies

CHEWY CHOCOLATE BARS

CRUST
    4   cups old-fashioned oats
  3/4   cup dark corn syrup
    1   cup firmly packed brown sugar
  2/3   cup butter or margarine, melted
  1/2   cup crunchy peanut butter
    2   teaspoons vanilla extract

TOPPING
    1   package (12 ounces)
          semisweet chocolate chips
  2/3   cup crunchy peanut butter
    1   cup coarsely chopped peanuts

Preheat oven to 350 degrees. For crust, combine oats, corn syrup, brown sugar, melted butter, peanut butter, and vanilla in a medium bowl. Press mixture into a lightly greased 9 x 13-inch baking pan. Bake 12 to 15 minutes; cool in pan.

For topping, melt chocolate chips and peanut butter in top of a double boiler over hot, not simmering, water. Stir in peanuts. Spread topping over crust. Cut into bars. Cover and chill until chocolate is firm. Store in refrigerator.
Yield: about 4 dozen bars

FRUITCAKE BITES

  1/2   cup dark rum
  1/4   cup golden raisins
  1/4   cup raisins
  1/4   cup butter or margarine,
          softened
  1/2   cup firmly packed brown sugar
    2   eggs, beaten
 1 1/2 cups all-purpose flour
 1 1/2 teaspoons baking soda
    1   teaspoon ground cinnamon
    1   teaspoon ground nutmeg
  1/2   teaspoon ground allspice
    3   tablespoons milk
  1/2   cup chopped green candied
          cherries
  1/2   cup chopped red candied
          cherries
  1/2   cup chopped dates
    2   cups chopped pecans

In a small bowl, combine rum and raisins. Let stand at room temperature 1 hour.

Preheat oven to 275 degrees. In a large bowl, cream butter and brown sugar until fluffy. Add eggs; beat until smooth. In a small bowl, combine flour, baking soda, and spices. Stir dry ingredients into creamed mixture. Stir in milk and raisin mixture. Stir in cherries, dates, and pecans. Fill paper-lined miniature muffin cups about two-thirds full. Bake 10 to 15 minutes or until top of muffin springs back when lightly touched. Transfer to a wire rack to cool. Store in an airtight container.
Yield: about 5 dozen muffins

Moist Fruitcake Bites (clockwise from top left) *feature the flavor of dark rum. Easy-to-make Chocolate Shortbread is a light and flaky confection. Guests will love the home-baked appeal of rich Chewy Chocolate Bars.*

Bourbon Pecan Balls, coated with dark chocolate, are a spirited treat. You'll also love scrumptious Toffee Cookies and Jessie's Brickly Cookies.

BOURBON PECAN BALLS

- 2 cups chopped pecans
- 3/4 cup bourbon
- 1/2 cup butter or margarine, softened
- 1 teaspoon vanilla extract
- 9 to 11 cups confectioners sugar
- 8 ounces unsweetened baking chocolate, chopped
- 8 ounces chocolate candy coating, chopped

Combine pecans and bourbon in an airtight container. Allow to stand at room temperature 48 hours, stirring occasionally.

In a large bowl, combine butter and vanilla. Stir in nuts. Gradually add confectioners sugar until mixture is stiff. Shape mixture into 3/4-inch balls. Place on a baking sheet lined with waxed paper; cover tightly with plastic wrap. Chill 1 hour.

Melt chocolate and candy coating in top of a double boiler over hot, not simmering, water. Dip balls into chocolate. Place on a baking sheet lined with waxed paper. Chill until chocolate hardens. Store in an airtight container in refrigerator.
Yield: about 10 dozen balls

TOFFEE COOKIES

- 1 cup butter or margarine, softened
- 3/4 cup granulated sugar
- 3/4 cup firmly packed brown sugar
- 2 eggs
- 1 tablespoon vanilla extract
- 2 1/4 cups all-purpose flour
- 1 teaspoon baking soda
- 1 teaspoon salt
- 2 cups coarsely chopped chocolate-covered English toffee bars

Preheat oven to 350 degrees. In a large bowl, cream butter and sugars until fluffy. Add eggs and vanilla; beat until smooth. In a medium bowl, stir together flour, baking soda, and salt. Add dry ingredients to creamed mixture; stir until a soft dough forms. Stir in toffee pieces. Drop by heaping teaspoonfuls 2 inches apart onto a greased baking sheet. Bake 8 to 10 minutes or until edges are lightly browned. Transfer to a wire rack to cool completely. Store in an airtight container.
Yield: about 6 1/2 dozen cookies

JESSIE'S BRICKLY COOKIES

- 1/2 cup butter or margarine, softened
- 1/2 cup vegetable shortening
- 1 cup sugar
- 2 eggs
- 2 teaspoons vanilla extract
- 4 1/2 cups all-purpose flour
- 1 teaspoon baking soda
- 1/2 teaspoon baking powder
- 1/2 teaspoon salt
- 1/2 cup buttermilk
  Sugar

In a large bowl, cream butter, shortening, and 1 cup sugar until fluffy. Add eggs and vanilla; beat until smooth. In a medium bowl, combine flour, baking soda, baking powder, and salt. Alternately add dry ingredients and buttermilk to creamed mixture. Stir until a soft dough forms. Divide dough into thirds and wrap in plastic wrap. Chill 2 hours.

Preheat oven to 375 degrees. On a lightly floured surface, use a floured rolling pin to roll out dough to 1/8-inch thickness. Use 1 5/8-inch and 2 1/4-inch star-shaped cookie cutters to cut out cookies. Transfer to an ungreased baking sheet. Sprinkle with sugar. Bake 5 to 7 minutes or until bottoms are lightly browned. Transfer cookies to a wire rack to cool. Store in an airtight container.
Yield: about 15 1/2 dozen cookies

TEACUP COOKIES

COOKIES

- 3/4 cup butter or margarine, softened
- 1/2 cup granulated sugar
- 1/2 cup confectioners sugar
- 1 egg
- 1 teaspoon almond extract
- 1/2 teaspoon vanilla extract
- 2 cups all-purpose flour
- 1/8 teaspoon salt

DECORATING ICING

- 2 1/2 cups confectioners sugar
- 2 1/2 to 3 tablespoons water
- 1/2 teaspoon almond extract
  Blue, green, and pink paste food coloring

GLAZE

- 2 1/2 cups confectioners sugar
- 2 1/2 to 3 tablespoons water
- 1 teaspoon almond extract

Trace teacup pattern onto stencil plastic; cut out. Preheat oven to 350 degrees. For cookies, cream butter and sugars in a medium bowl until fluffy. Add egg and extracts; beat until smooth. In a small bowl, combine flour and salt. Add dry ingredients to creamed mixture; stir until a soft dough forms. On a lightly floured surface, use a floured rolling pin to roll out dough to 1/8-inch thickness. Use pattern and a sharp knife to cut out cookies. Transfer to a greased baking sheet. Bake 8 to 10 minutes or until bottoms are lightly browned. Transfer cookies to a wire rack to cool.

For decorating icing, combine confectioners sugar, water, and almond extract in a small bowl; stir until smooth. Divide icing into 3 small bowls; tint light blue, green, and pink. Spoon icing into pastry bags fitted with small round tips. Using blue icing, pipe outline of teacup onto each cookie. Allow icing to harden. Cover tips with plastic wrap; set aside.

For glaze, combine confectioners sugar, water, and almond extract in a small bowl; stir until smooth (icing should be thin enough to flow easily). Spoon glaze into a pastry bag fitted with a round tip. Pipe glaze onto each cookie, filling in outline. Allow glaze to harden.

Pipe designs onto glaze using remaining decorating icing. Allow icing to harden. Store in a single layer in an airtight container.

Yield: about 2 dozen cookies

Resembling delicate porcelain china, our tasty Teacup Cookies are decorated with an almond glaze and piped icing.

Cut in a wreath shape, crispy Butterscotch Cookies are embellished with red icing bows and green candies.

BUTTERSCOTCH COOKIES

1/2 cup butter or margarine, softened
1/3 cup granulated sugar
1/3 cup firmly packed brown sugar
1 egg
1 teaspoon vanilla extract
1 cup butterscotch chips, melted
2 1/3 cups all-purpose flour
3/4 teaspoon baking soda
Purchased red decorating icing
Green candy-coated chocolate pieces

Preheat oven to 375 degrees. In a large bowl, cream butter and sugars until fluffy. Add egg and vanilla, mixing until smooth. Stir in melted butterscotch chips. In a medium bowl, combine flour and baking soda. Stir dry ingredients into creamed mixture. On a lightly floured surface, use a floured rolling pin to roll out dough to 1/4-inch thickness. Use a doughnut cutter to cut out cookies. Transfer to a greased baking sheet. Bake 8 to 10 minutes or until brown. Cool completely on a wire rack. Using a leaf tip and icing, pipe a bow onto each cookie. Press a candy-coated piece on each bow before icing hardens. Let icing harden. Store in an airtight container.
Yield: about 2 1/2 dozen 3-inch cookies

CREAMY CHOCOLATE CARAMELS

2 cups sugar
1 1/2 cups whipping cream, divided
1 cup light corn syrup
1/4 cup butter
4 ounces unsweetened baking chocolate, chopped
1 teaspoon vanilla extract

Line a 9-inch square baking pan with aluminum foil, extending foil over 2 sides of pan; grease foil. Butter sides of a heavy Dutch oven. Combine sugar, 3/4 cup whipping cream, corn syrup, and butter in Dutch oven. Stirring constantly, cook over medium-low heat until sugar dissolves. Add chocolate; stir until melted. Using a pastry brush dipped in hot water, wash down any sugar crystals on sides of pan. Attach a candy thermometer to pan, making sure thermometer does not touch bottom of pan. Increase heat to medium; continue to stir and bring mixture to a boil. Gradually stir in remaining 3/4 cup whipping cream. Stirring frequently without touching sides of pan, cook until mixture reaches firm-ball stage (approximately 242 to 248 degrees). Test about 1/2 teaspoon mixture in ice water. Mixture will roll into a firm ball in ice water but will flatten if pressed when removed from water. Remove from heat and stir in vanilla. Pour mixture into prepared pan. Cool several hours at room temperature.

Use ends of foil to lift candy from pan. Use a lightly oiled heavy knife to cut candy into 1-inch squares. Wrap in waxed paper and store in a cool place.
Yield: about 6 1/2 dozen caramels

HOLIDAY CANDY TWISTS

You will need someone to help you pull this candy.

2 cups sugar
2/3 cup light corn syrup
1/2 cup water
2 tablespoons butter or margarine
1/4 teaspoon cream of tartar
1 teaspoon vanilla extract, divided
Red and green liquid food coloring

Butter sides of a 3-quart heavy saucepan. Combine sugar, corn syrup, water, butter, and cream of tartar in pan. Stirring constantly, cook over medium-low heat until sugar dissolves. Using a pastry brush dipped in hot water, wash down any sugar crystals on sides of pan. Attach a

A firmer version of old-fashioned taffy, festive Holiday Candy Twists (right) are made by pulling the confection into long ropes that are then cut into individual pieces. Bursting with fudgy goodness, Creamy Chocolate Caramels are too tasty to resist!

candy thermometer to pan, making sure thermometer does not touch bottom of pan. Increase heat to medium high and bring mixture to a boil. Cook, without stirring, until mixture reaches upper limits of hard-ball stage (approximately 268 degrees). Test about $1/2$ teaspoon mixture in ice water. Mixture will roll into a hard ball in ice water and will remain hard when removed from water. Remove from heat; immediately pour half of candy into a warmed saucepan. Stir $1/2$ teaspoon vanilla and about $1/8$ teaspoon red or green food coloring into each half of candy. Immediately pour each color of candy onto a cool, buttered surface. Allow to cool enough to handle. With greased hands, pull candy into a long rope. Fold candy back onto itself, twist, and pull again. Continue the pulling, twisting, and folding motion until candy lightens in color, begins to hold a shape, and is no longer sticky. Using a twisting motion, pull into smaller $1/2$-inch-diameter ropes. Use kitchen scissors to cut ropes into $3/4$-inch-long pieces. Allow pieces to cool completely. Wrap in waxed paper. Store in an airtight container.

Yield: about $1 1/4$ pounds candy

Two luscious layers make Chocolate-Butterscotch Candy extra special. Rich Pineapple Cream Candy is a sweet blend of fruit, marshmallows, and walnuts.

CHOCOLATE-BUTTERSCOTCH CANDY

1 package (11 ounces) butterscotch chips
1 package (12 ounces) semisweet chocolate chips
1/2 cup raisins
1/2 cup chopped pecans

Line a 7 x 11-inch pan with waxed paper. In separate small saucepans, melt butterscotch and chocolate chips over low heat, stirring constantly. Remove from heat. Stir raisins into butterscotch chips; spread into prepared pan. Stir pecans into chocolate chips; spread over butterscotch mixture. Allow candy to harden. Cut into 1-inch squares. Store in an airtight container in a cool, dry place.

Yield: about 5 dozen pieces candy

PINEAPPLE CREAM CANDY

1 cup granulated sugar
1/2 cup firmly packed brown sugar
1/2 cup undrained crushed pineapple
1 cup chopped walnuts
12 large marshmallows
1 teaspoon lemon extract

Butter sides of a 2-quart heavy saucepan. Combine sugars and pineapple in pan. Stirring constantly, cook over medium-low heat until sugars dissolve. Using a pastry brush dipped in hot water, wash down any sugar crystals on sides of pan. Attach candy thermometer to pan, making sure thermometer does not touch bottom of pan. Increase heat to medium and bring to a boil. Cook, without stirring, until mixture reaches

200 degrees. Stir in walnuts. Continue to cook until mixture reaches soft-ball stage (approximately 234 to 240 degrees). Test about 1/2 teaspoon mixture in ice water. Mixture should easily form a ball in ice water but flatten when removed from water. Remove from heat; add marshmallows (do not stir). When marshmallows start to melt, add lemon extract and stir until mixture begins to thicken. Quickly drop tablespoonfuls 1 inch apart onto buttered aluminum foil. Cool completely. Store in an airtight container.

Yield: about 3 dozen pieces candy

FRUIT CANDIES

1 2/3 cups sugar
2/3 cup light corn syrup
1/2 cup water
4 drops **each** lime-flavored and raspberry-flavored oils
1/8 teaspoon **each** green and red liquid food colorings
2 ounces vanilla candy coating

In a heavy medium saucepan, combine sugar, corn syrup, and water. Stirring constantly, cook over medium-low heat until sugar dissolves. Using a pastry brush dipped in hot water, wash down any sugar crystals on sides of pan. Attach a candy thermometer to pan, making sure thermometer does not touch bottom of pan. Increase heat to medium-high and bring to a boil. Cook, without stirring, until mixture reaches soft-crack stage (approximately 270 to 290 degrees). Test about 1/2 teaspoon mixture in ice water. Mixture will form hard threads in ice water but will soften when removed from water. Remove from heat; immediately pour half of mixture into a warmed saucepan. Stir lime oil and green food coloring into half of mixture; stir raspberry oil and red food coloring into remaining mixture. Pour each flavored candy into lightly greased 1 3/8-inch-diameter candy molds. Allow candy to cool completely; unmold onto a wire rack with waxed paper underneath.

Melt candy coating in a heavy small saucepan over low heat. Spoon candy coating into a resealable plastic bag. Snip off 1 corner of bag and drizzle candy coating over candies. Allow coating to harden. Store in an airtight container.

Yield: about 5¹/₂ dozen pieces candy

HAWAIIAN FUDGE

- 1 can (15¹/₄ ounces) crushed pineapple in juice
- 4 cups sugar
- 1 cup whipping cream
- 2 tablespoons butter or margarine
- 1 teaspoon vanilla extract
- 1 cup chopped macadamia nuts
- ¹/₂ cup flaked coconut
- 1 tablespoon chopped crystallized ginger

Drain pineapple (do not squeeze dry); reserve juice. Line an 8-inch square baking pan with aluminum foil, extending foil over 2 sides of pan; grease foil. Butter sides of a heavy large saucepan. Combine sugar, whipping cream, pineapple, and 2 tablespoons reserved pineapple juice in saucepan. Stirring constantly, cook over medium-low heat until sugar dissolves. Using a pastry brush dipped in hot water, wash down any sugar crystals on sides of pan. Attach a candy thermometer to pan, making sure thermometer does not touch bottom of pan. Increase heat to medium and bring mixture to a boil. Cook, without stirring, until mixture reaches soft-ball stage (approximately 234 to 240 degrees). Test about ¹/₂ teaspoon mixture in ice water. Mixture will easily form a ball in ice water but will flatten when removed from water. Remove from heat. Add butter and vanilla; do not stir. Place pan in 2 inches of cold water in sink. Cool to approximately 110 degrees. Remove from sink. Beat fudge until it thickens and begins to lose its gloss. Stir in macadamia nuts, coconut, and ginger. Pour into prepared pan. Cool completely.

Use ends of foil to lift fudge from pan. Cut into 1-inch squares. Store in an airtight container in refrigerator.

Yield: about 4 dozen pieces fudge

Enhanced with lime and raspberry flavorings, Fruit Candies (in tin) are drizzled with vanilla candy coating. A tropical paradise for the taste buds, Hawaiian Fudge is a fruity delight loaded with bits of sun-ripened pineapple, crunchy macadamia nuts, and flaked coconut.

Baked in festive shapes and colorfully decorated, Star and Tree Butter Cookies and Reindeer Cookies make fun additions to a cookie swap.

REINDEER COOKIES

- ¹/₂ cup butter or margarine, softened
- ¹/₂ cup sugar
- ¹/₂ teaspoon vanilla extract
- ¹/₂ teaspoon almond extract
- 1¹/₃ cups all-purpose flour
- ¹/₂ cup finely ground walnuts
- ¹/₄ teaspoon salt
  Purchased white decorating icing
  Small red cinnamon candies

Trace reindeer pattern onto stencil plastic; cut out. Preheat oven to 350 degrees. In a large bowl, cream butter and sugar until fluffy. Stir in extracts. In a small bowl, combine flour, walnuts, and salt. Add flour mixture to creamed mixture; stir until a soft dough forms. On a lightly floured surface, use a floured rolling pin to roll out dough to ¹/₄-inch thickness. Use pattern and a sharp knife to cut out cookies. Transfer to a greased baking sheet. Bake 8 to 10 minutes or until edges are lightly browned. Cool on baking sheet 2 minutes. Transfer cookies to a wire rack to cool completely. Refer to photo and use a small round tip to pipe icing onto cookies. Use a small amount of icing to secure a candy on each cookie for nose. Allow icing to harden. Store in an airtight container.

Yield: about 1 dozen cookies

STAR AND TREE BUTTER COOKIES

COOKIES

- 1 cup butter or margarine, softened
- 1¹/₂ cups sugar
- 1 egg
- 1 teaspoon vanilla extract
- 2³/₄ cups all-purpose flour
- ¹/₄ teaspoon salt

ICING

- 3³/₄ cups confectioners sugar
- ¹/₂ cup plus 1 tablespoon milk
- ¹/₂ teaspoon almond extract
  Green paste food coloring
  Purchased white, green, and red decorating icing
  Small red cinnamon candies
  Purchased red sugar crystals

For cookies, preheat oven to 375 degrees. In a large bowl, cream butter and sugar until fluffy. Add egg and vanilla; stir until smooth. In a medium bowl, combine flour and salt. Add dry ingredients to creamed mixture; stir until a soft dough forms. On a lightly floured surface, use a floured rolling pin to roll out dough to 1/4-inch thickness. Use desired tree- and star-shaped cookie cutters to cut out cookies. Transfer tree- and star-shaped cookies to separate greased baking sheets. Bake tree-shaped cookies 8 to 10 minutes or until edges are lightly browned. Bake star-shaped cookies 6 to 8 minutes or until edges are lightly browned. Transfer cookies to a wire rack with waxed paper underneath to cool completely.

For icing, combine confectioners sugar, milk, and almond extract in a small bowl; stir until smooth. Tint green. Ice some of the tree-shaped cookies green. Allow icing to harden. Use a small round tip to pipe white decorating icing onto green-iced tree-shaped cookies for snow. Use a small amount of white icing to secure a red candy to top of each tree. Allow icing to harden. Use a small round tip to pipe green decorating icing onto remaining tree-shaped cookies. Before icing hardens, press a red candy on top of each cookie. Allow icing to harden. Use a small round tip to pipe red icing onto star-shaped cookies. Before icing hardens, sprinkle red sugar on star-shaped cookies. Shake off excess sugar. Allow icing to harden. Store in an airtight container.
Yield: about 3 1/2 dozen 3 to 5-inch cookies

SANTA CUPCAKES

CUPCAKES
- 1/2 cup butter or margarine, softened
- 3/4 cup firmly packed brown sugar
- 2 eggs
- 1 teaspoon vanilla extract
- 1 cup milk
- 1/2 cup frozen apple juice concentrate, thawed
- 2 1/4 cups all-purpose flour

Scrumptious chocolate Santa Cupcakes are adorned with icing, candied cherries, and raisins to resemble the jolly old gent's cheerful face.

- 1/2 cup cocoa
- 3/4 teaspoon baking soda
- 1/2 teaspoon salt

FROSTING
- 3/4 cup butter or margarine, softened
- 6 3/4 cups confectioners sugar
- 1/2 cup milk
- 1 teaspoon vanilla extract
  Candied cherries, halved
  Raisins
  Red paste food coloring

For cupcakes, preheat oven to 375 degrees. In a large bowl, cream butter and brown sugar until fluffy. Add eggs and vanilla; stir until smooth. Stir in milk and apple juice. In a medium bowl, combine flour, cocoa, baking soda, and salt. Add dry ingredients to creamed mixture; stir until well blended. Spoon batter into a paper-lined muffin pan, filling each cup three-fourths full. Bake 18 to 20 minutes or until a toothpick inserted in center of cake comes out clean. Transfer to a wire rack to cool completely.

For frosting, combine butter, confectioners sugar, milk, and vanilla; stir until smooth. Spread a thin layer of frosting over tops of cupcakes. Press cherries and raisins onto frosting for noses and eyes. Transfer 1 cup remaining frosting to a small bowl; tint red. Spoon red and remaining white frosting into separate pastry bags fitted with large star tips. Pipe red frosting onto cupcakes for caps. Pipe white frosting onto cupcakes for trim and beards. Store in an airtight container.
Yield: about 1 1/2 dozen cupcakes

HOLIDAY OPEN HOUSE

When the presents are wrapped and tucked away until Christmas, the tree is a-twinkle with lights, and the house is decked in holiday cheer, it's time to invite those special friends over for a merry open house. The menu will be no-fuss with these scrumptious recipes, which include a bounty of beverages and fabulous finger foods, as well as heartier fare. You'll also find lots of snacks to please your younger guests. Hosting a holiday gathering has never been easier!

An icy cold refreshment, Strawberry Wine Punch (from left, recipes on page 32) is a sweet accompaniment for these appetizers. Rolled in bread crumbs and baked until golden brown, Savory Party Bites are tasty morsels. Red pepper flavors melt-in-your-mouth Sesame-Parmesan Rounds.

SAVORY PARTY BITES

(Shown on pages 30 and 31)

- 1 pound hot pork sausage
- 1 package (8 ounces) cream cheese, softened
- 1/2 cup finely chopped onion
- 1/3 cup chopped fresh parsley
- 3 tablespoons prepared mustard
- 1/4 teaspoon garlic powder
- 1 can (10 ounces) chopped sauerkraut, drained
- 4 1/2 cups all-purpose baking mix
- 1 1/4 cups bread crumbs
- 2 1/2 teaspoons paprika

Process uncooked sausage, cream cheese, onion, parsley, mustard, and garlic powder in a food processor just until blended. Add sauerkraut; pulse process until blended. Transfer mixture to a large bowl. Stir in baking mix. Cover and chill 1 hour.

Preheat oven to 350 degrees. In a small bowl, combine bread crumbs and paprika. Shape sausage mixture into 1-inch balls. Roll each ball in bread crumb mixture. Place on a lightly greased baking sheet. Bake 23 to 26 minutes or until golden brown; serve warm.

Yield: about 8 dozen appetizers

SESAME-PARMESAN ROUNDS (Shown on page 31)

- 2 cups all-purpose flour
- 1/2 teaspoon ground red pepper
- 1/8 teaspoon salt
- 1 cup butter, softened
- 1 cup freshly grated Parmesan cheese
- 1 egg white
- 1 teaspoon water
- 1/4 cup sesame seed, toasted

Preheat oven to 350 degrees. In a medium bowl, combine flour, red pepper, and salt; set aside. In a large bowl, combine butter and cheese; beat until well blended. Add dry ingredients to creamed mixture; stir until well blended. On a lightly floured surface, use a floured rolling pin to roll out

Store-bought taco seasoning mix gives Fiesta Snack Mix zesty appeal.

dough to 1/8-inch thickness. Use a 1 1/2-inch biscuit cutter to cut out dough. Transfer to a greased baking sheet. In a small bowl, beat egg white and water until blended. Brush dough with egg white mixture and sprinkle with sesame seed. Bake 12 to 14 minutes or until bottoms are lightly browned. Serve warm. To reheat crackers, place in a 325-degree oven about 2 minutes.

Yield: about 8 dozen crackers

STRAWBERRY WINE PUNCH

(Shown on pages 30 and 31)

- 1/2 cup sugar
- 1/4 cup water
- 2 packages (10 ounces each) frozen sweetened sliced strawberries, partially thawed
- 2 bottles (750 ml each) red wine, chilled
- 1 bottle (2 liters) lemon-lime soda, chilled

In a small saucepan, combine sugar and water over medium-high heat. Stirring frequently, bring to a boil. Remove from heat and cool. Cover and

chill syrup until ready to serve.

To serve, place strawberries in a 1 1/2-gallon container. Pour wine and lemon-lime soda over strawberries; carefully stir to break up strawberries. Sweeten punch to taste by adding 1 tablespoon syrup at a time; stir well after each addition. Serve immediately.

Yield: about 16 cups punch

FIESTA SNACK MIX

- 1 can (7 1/2 ounces) corn chips
- 1 can (12 ounces) salted mixed nuts
- 1/4 cup butter or margarine, melted
- 1/4 cup grated Parmesan cheese
- 2 teaspoons taco seasoning mix

Preheat oven to 325 degrees. In a large bowl, combine corn chips and nuts. In a small bowl, combine melted butter, cheese, and taco seasoning mix. Pour over corn chip mixture. Stir until well coated. Spread mixture evenly on a baking sheet. Bake 12 minutes. Cool completely. Store in an airtight container.

Yield: about 6 cups snack mix

Cool, frothy Strawberry Fizz is bursting with berry flavor. Pepperoni-topped Layered Pizza Dip is a sure-fire crowd pleaser!

STRAWBERRY FIZZ

3 packages (10 ounces each) frozen sweetened sliced strawberries
3 cartons (8 ounces each) strawberry yogurt
2 tablespoons sugar
4 cans (12 ounces each) strawberry-flavored soft drink, chilled

Process frozen strawberries, yogurt, and sugar in a food processor until smooth. Spoon strawberry mixture into a punch bowl; stir in soft drink. Serve immediately.
Yield: about 16 cups punch

LAYERED PIZZA DIP

1 package (8 ounces) cream cheese, softened
$1/2$ cup sour cream
$1/4$ cup freshly grated Parmesan cheese
$1/2$ teaspoon garlic salt
$1/2$ cup prepared pizza sauce
$3/4$ cup shredded mozzarella cheese
1 package ($3^1/2$ ounces) sliced pepperoni, finely chopped
Toasted pita bread wedges to serve

Preheat oven to 350 degrees. In a small bowl, beat cream cheese until fluffy. Stir in sour cream, Parmesan cheese, and garlic salt. Spread into a lightly greased 9-inch pie plate. Spread pizza sauce over cream cheese mixture. Sprinkle mozzarella cheese over pizza sauce and top with pepperoni. Bake about 20 minutes or until heated through. Serve warm with pita bread.
Yield: about 3 cups dip

CORN SALAD WITH ROASTED GARLIC DRESSING

- 1 head garlic (about 10 to 14 cloves)
  Olive oil
- 2/3 cup mayonnaise
- 1/2 cup chopped fresh parsley
- 1 tablespoon Greek seasoning
- 4 cans (15¼ ounces each) whole kernel yellow corn, drained
- 2 cups chopped sweet red pepper
- 1½ cups chopped green onions

Preheat oven to 400 degrees. To roast garlic, slightly trim tops of garlic cloves. Place garlic head on aluminum foil. Drizzle a small amount of oil on cut edges; wrap in foil. Bake 1 hour. Cool completely.

Press garlic pulp out of each clove and mash in a small bowl. Add mayonnaise, parsley, and Greek seasoning; stir until well blended. In a large bowl, combine corn, red pepper, and green onions; toss with garlic dressing. Cover and chill 2 hours before serving.

Yield: about 9 cups salad

FOUR-CHEESE QUICHES

- 1 container (15 ounces) ricotta cheese
- 11 ounces cream cheese, softened
- 9 eggs
- 3 tablespoons chopped fresh parsley
- 1 tablespoon stone-ground mustard
- 1/3 cup freshly grated Parmesan cheese
- 2 tablespoons all-purpose flour
- 1 teaspoon baking powder
- 1/2 teaspoon salt
- 3 cups (12 ounces) shredded Jarlsberg cheese

Preheat oven to 350 degrees. In a large bowl, beat ricotta cheese and cream cheese until blended. Beat in eggs, parsley, and mustard. In a small bowl, combine Parmesan cheese, flour, baking powder, and salt. Stir dry ingredients into egg mixture; beat until well blended. Stir in Jarlsberg cheese. Pour into 2 greased 9-inch deep-dish pie plates. Bake 33 to 38 minutes or until a knife inserted near center of quiche comes out clean. Allow to stand 10 minutes before serving.

Yield: 2 quiches, about 8 servings each

Corn Salad with Roasted Garlic Dressing delights the senses with a confetti of veggies tossed in a zippy dressing. Four-Cheese Quiche is incredibly light and flavorful.

Thinly sliced ham is a tasty surprise rolled inside hearty Peppered Cheese Biscuits!

PEPPERED CHEESE BISCUITS

2/3 cup grated Parmesan cheese
1 1/2 teaspoons ground black pepper
2 cups all-purpose flour
1 tablespoon baking powder
1 teaspoon baking soda
1/2 teaspoon salt
1/8 teaspoon ground red pepper
1 teaspoon dried minced onion
1/4 cup chilled butter or margarine, cut into pieces
2/3 cup sour cream
1/3 cup half and half
1/2 pound thinly sliced deli ham
2 tablespoons butter or margarine, melted

Process cheese and black pepper 5 to 10 seconds in a food processor until well blended. Sift flour, baking powder, baking soda, salt, and red pepper into a large bowl. Stir cheese mixture and onion into dry ingredients. Using a pastry blender or 2 knives, cut chilled butter into dry ingredients until mixture resembles coarse meal. Stir in sour cream and half and half; knead until a soft dough forms. On a lightly floured surface, use a floured rolling pin to roll out dough to a 1/4-inch-thick rectangle. Place ham on dough. Beginning at 1 long edge, roll up

dough jellyroll style. Pinch seam to seal. Wrap in plastic wrap and chill 1 hour.

Preheat oven to 450 degrees. Use a sharp knife to cut roll into 1/2-inch-thick slices. Transfer to a greased baking sheet. Brush with melted butter. Bake 10 to 12 minutes or until golden brown. Serve warm.

Yield: about 2 dozen biscuits

OVEN-BAKED MINESTRONE SOUP

1½ pounds stew beef, cut into small
    pieces
1 cup chopped onion
2 cloves garlic, minced
2 tablespoons olive oil
1 teaspoon salt
1 teaspoon ground black pepper
3 cans (14½ ounces each) beef
    broth
2¾ cups water
1 can (16 ounces) kidney beans
1 can (14½ ounces) diced
    stewed tomatoes
1½ cups thinly sliced carrots
1 can (6 ounces) whole pitted
    ripe olives
2 cups sliced zucchini
1 cup uncooked small elbow
    macaroni
½ teaspoon dried basil leaves
¼ teaspoon dried thyme leaves
¼ teaspoon dried oregano leaves
¼ teaspoon dried rosemary leaves
¼ teaspoon ground savory
    Freshly shredded Parmesan
    cheese to serve

Preheat oven to 400 degrees. In a large ovenproof Dutch oven, combine beef, onion, garlic, oil, salt, and pepper. Stirring occasionally, bake uncovered 45 minutes. Leaving soup in oven, reduce heat to 350 degrees. Combine beef broth and water in a 2-quart microwave-safe container. Microwave on high power (100%) 10 minutes or until broth mixture begins to boil; add to beef mixture. Stir in undrained beans, undrained tomatoes, carrots, and undrained olives. Cover and bake about 2 hours or until meat is tender. Stir in zucchini, macaroni, and herbs; cover and bake 30 minutes longer or until vegetables are tender. To serve, sprinkle each serving with cheese.
Yield: about 15 cups soup

OLD-FASHIONED YEAST ROLLS

1 cup warm milk
1 cup warm water
2 packages dry yeast
1 tablespoon sugar
4 to 5 cups all-purpose flour,
    divided
3 tablespoons butter or margarine,
    melted
2 teaspoons salt
    Vegetable cooking spray
1 egg, beaten
1 tablespoon milk

In a large bowl, combine warm milk, water, yeast, sugar, and 1 cup flour. Beat mixture until well blended and smooth. Cover and let rise in a warm place (80 to 85 degrees) 1 hour or until doubled in size.

Stir melted butter and salt into yeast mixture. Add 3 cups flour; stir until a soft dough forms. Turn dough onto a lightly floured surface. Knead about 5 minutes or until dough becomes smooth and elastic, using additional flour as necessary. Place in a large bowl sprayed with cooking spray, turning once to coat top of dough. Cover and let rise in a warm place about 2 hours or until tripled in size.

Turn dough onto a lightly floured surface and punch down. Shape dough into 2-inch rolls. Place 2 inches apart on a greased baking sheet. Spray tops of rolls with cooking spray. Cover and let rise in a warm place 1 hour or until almost doubled in size.

Preheat oven to 375 degrees. In a small bowl, combine egg and milk. Brush rolls with egg mixture. Bake 20 to 25 minutes or until rolls are lightly browned. Serve warm or transfer to a wire rack to cool completely.
Yield: about 2 dozen rolls

CRUNCHY BREADSTICK STREAMERS

2 cans (2.8 ounces each) French-
    fried onions, crushed
1 egg, lightly beaten
2 tablespoons milk
1 can (11 ounces) refrigerated
    breadstick dough

Preheat oven to 350 degrees. Place crushed onions on a piece of aluminum foil. In a small bowl, combine egg and milk. Without separating strips, unroll dough onto a flat surface. Cut dough in half crosswise. Brush both sides of dough pieces with egg mixture. Separate dough at perforations to form 16 strips. Roll each strip in onions, lightly pressing onions into dough. Place on a greased baking sheet; twist ends in opposite directions. Bake 13 to 15 minutes or until golden brown. Serve warm.
Yield: 16 breadsticks

Serve Oven-Baked Minestrone Soup for a perfect winter warmer! Old-fashioned Yeast Rolls are just like the ones Grandma would have made. For a flavorful change from dinner rolls, try easy-to-make Crunchy Breadstick Streamers.

A blend of saffron and other spices, along with yogurt and ground peanuts, gives make-ahead Saffron Shrimp international flair.

SAFFRON SHRIMP

1 can (10½ ounces) chicken broth
½ teaspoon crushed saffron threads
1 tablespoon olive oil
1 large onion, finely chopped
4 cloves garlic, minced
1 cup unsalted roasted peanuts
1 cup plain yogurt
2 teaspoons chopped crystallized
    ginger
2 teaspoons ground coriander
1 teaspoon ground cumin
1 teaspoon ground cardamom
½ teaspoon salt
¼ teaspoon ground black pepper
2 packages (6 ounces each)
    frozen cooked and peeled
    shrimp, thawed and drained
3 cups cooked white rice

Preheat oven to 375 degrees. In a small saucepan, heat chicken broth over medium heat until boiling; remove from heat. Stir in saffron; set aside. In a small skillet, heat oil over medium heat. Sauté onion and garlic until browned. Process peanuts in a large food processor until finely ground. Add onion mixture, broth mixture, and next 7 ingredients to food processor; process until well blended. Transfer to a large bowl; stir in shrimp and rice. Pour into a 1½-quart casserole dish. Cover and bake 20 to 25 minutes or until heated through. Serve warm.
Yield: 6 to 8 servings

HAM AND SWISS PARTY LOAVES

½ cup butter or margarine, softened
3 tablespoons Dijon-style mustard
2 tablespoons Worcestershire sauce
1½ tablespoons dried minced onion
1 package (16 ounces) 2 small
    French bread loaves
8 ounces thinly sliced ham
6 ounces thinly sliced Swiss cheese

In a small bowl, combine butter, mustard, Worcestershire sauce, and onion until well blended. Split loaves in half lengthwise. Spread inside of

These finger sandwiches taste like they came from the deli! Bake up Ham and Swiss or Roast Beef and Cheddar Party Loaves to satisfy hearty appetites.

each loaf with butter mixture. Layer bottom halves with ham and cheese. Place top halves on loaves. Wrap in aluminum foil and store in refrigerator until ready to serve.

To serve, bake loaves in foil in a 350-degree oven 15 to 20 minutes or until bread is warm and cheese is melted. Cut into 1-inch slices and serve warm.
Yield: 2 party loaves, about 12 servings each

ROAST BEEF AND CHEDDAR PARTY LOAVES

⅓ cup mayonnaise
3 tablespoons Dijon-style mustard
2½ tablespoons Worcestershire sauce
1 tablespoon dried minced onion
1 package (16 ounces) 2 small
    French bread loaves
8 ounces thinly sliced roast beef
6 ounces thinly sliced Cheddar
    cheese

In a small bowl, combine mayonnaise, mustard, Worcestershire sauce, and onion until well blended. Split loaves in half lengthwise. Spread inside of each loaf with mayonnaise mixture. Layer bottom halves with roast beef and cheese. Place top halves on loaves. Wrap in aluminum foil and store in refrigerator until ready to serve.

To serve, bake loaves in foil in a 350-degree oven 15 to 20 minutes or until bread is warm and cheese is melted. Cut into 1-inch slices and serve warm.
Yield: 2 party loaves, about 12 servings each

ORANGE-PINEAPPLE PUNCH

Punch must be made 1 day in advance.

- 2 quarts water
- 2 cans (20 ounces each) crushed pineapple in juice, undrained
- 3 cups sugar
- 3 ripe bananas, mashed
- 1 can (12 ounces) frozen orange juice concentrate, thawed
- 1 can (6 ounces) frozen lemonade concentrate, thawed
- 1 package (0.14 ounce) unsweetened orange-flavored soft drink mix
- 1 bottle (1 liter) ginger ale, chilled
- 1 jar (10 ounces) maraschino cherries, drained

In a 6-quart container, combine first 7 ingredients. Place punch in a covered container and freeze.

Remove punch from freezer 4 hours before serving to partially thaw.

To serve, break into chunks. Add ginger ale and cherries; stir until slushy.

Yield: about 20 cups punch

"BEARY" CHRISTMAS POPCORN SNACKS

- 16 cups popped popcorn
- 4 cups miniature marshmallows
- 1/4 cup butter or margarine
- 2 tablespoons milk
- 1/2 cup smooth peanut butter
- 1 tablespoon vanilla extract
- 1 teaspoon salt
  - Semisweet chocolate mini chips
  - Small red cinnamon candies
  - Ribbon to decorate

Place popcorn in a very large bowl. In a medium saucepan, combine marshmallows, butter, and milk. Stirring constantly, cook over low heat until marshmallows are melted. Remove from heat and stir in peanut butter, vanilla, and salt. Pour

"Beary" Christmas Popcorn Snacks are shaped in a mold and decorated with candies. Slushy Orange-Pineapple Punch has a fruity flavor that kids will love.

marshmallow mixture over popcorn and stir until evenly coated. With lightly greased hands, press about 1/2 cup popcorn mixture into a 4 1/2-inch-high bear-shaped mold. Transfer to waxed paper. Press 2 chocolate chips and 1 candy onto popcorn bear for eyes and nose. Repeat with remaining popcorn mixture, chocolate chips, and candies. Cool completely. Tie ribbon around neck of each bear. Store in an airtight container.

Yield: about 17 popcorn snacks

ARTICHOKE-BRIE SPREAD

- 2 jars (6 ounces each) marinated artichoke hearts, drained and divided
- 1 package (8 ounces) cream cheese, softened
- 1 cup mayonnaise
- 2 tablespoons chopped green onion
- 1/2 teaspoon dried oregano leaves, crushed
- 1/2 teaspoon salt
- 1/4 teaspoon ground black pepper
- 2 packages (4 1/2 ounces each) Brie cheese, cut into small pieces
  Fresh parsley to garnish
  Crackers or bread to serve

Preheat oven to 375 degrees. Reserving 1 artichoke heart, coarsely chop remaining artichoke hearts. In a large bowl, combine chopped artichoke hearts, cream cheese, mayonnaise, onion, oregano, salt, and pepper. Stir in Brie cheese. Spoon into a greased 9-inch pie plate. Bake 15 to 20 minutes or until bubbly. For garnish, cut reserved artichoke heart in half. Place artichoke halves and parsley on top of spread. Serve hot with crackers or bread.

Yield: about 3 1/2 cups spread

Bites of Shrimp Pâté are topped with sweet pepper stars and served on cucumber slices. Creamy, cheesy Artichoke-Brie Spread (not shown) is an especially delicious hot spread.

SHRIMP PÂTÉ

- 1 package (8 ounces) cream cheese, softened
- 8 ounces shrimp, cooked, peeled, and deveined
- 1 cup (4 ounces) shredded Cheddar cheese
- 3 tablespoons Dijon-style mustard
- 2 teaspoons prepared horseradish
- 1/2 teaspoon dried dill weed
- 1/2 teaspoon garlic powder
- 1/2 teaspoon salt
- 1/4 teaspoon ground black pepper
- 1/4 teaspoon onion powder
- 3 large cucumbers, thinly sliced
  Sweet red pepper and fresh parsley to garnish

Process cream cheese, shrimp, Cheddar cheese, mustard, horseradish, dill weed, garlic powder, salt, black pepper, and onion powder in a food processor until shrimp are finely chopped. Cover and refrigerate until well chilled. Shape into 1/2-inch balls and place on cucumber slices.

To garnish, use a star-shaped aspic cutter to cut out stars from red pepper; press stars and parsley into pâté. Store in an airtight container in refrigerator.

Yield: about 9 dozen appetizers

Spiced with a hint of red pepper, Sesame Seed Snack Crackers are delightful alone or served with cheese slices.

SESAME SEED SNACK CRACKERS

1½ cups quick-cooking oats
1 cup all-purpose flour
½ cup wheat germ
2 tablespoons sugar
1 teaspoon salt
¼ teaspoon ground red pepper
¼ cup chilled butter or margarine,
  cut into pieces
½ cup water
¼ cup sesame oil
2 tablespoons sesame seed,
  divided

Preheat oven to 350 degrees. In a large bowl, combine oats, flour, wheat germ, sugar, salt, and red pepper. Using a pastry blender or 2 knives, cut in butter until mixture resembles coarse meal. Add water and oil; stir until a soft dough forms. Divide dough in half. On a greased baking sheet, use a floured rolling pin to roll out half of dough into a 10 x 14-inch rectangle. Sprinkle

1 tablespoon sesame seed evenly over dough and use a rolling pin to press seed into dough. Use a sharp knife or pizza cutter to cut dough into 2-inch squares. Repeat for remaining dough and sesame seed. Bake 15 to 20 minutes or until edges are light brown and crackers are crisp. Cool completely on a wire rack. Store in an airtight container.
Yield: about 6 dozen crackers

Perfect for party-time snacking, miniature loaves of Swiss Cheese Bread have a mellow, nutty flavor.

SWISS CHEESE BREAD

4 cups all-purpose flour
2 tablespoons sugar
1 tablespoon baking powder
1½ teaspoons salt
½ cup chilled butter or margarine,
    cut into pieces
4 cups (16 ounces) shredded
    Swiss cheese
1 tablespoon dried dill weed
2 cups milk
2 eggs

Preheat oven to 400 degrees. In a large bowl, combine flour, sugar, baking powder, and salt. Using a pastry blender or 2 knives, cut in butter until mixture resembles coarse meal. Stir in cheese and dill weed. In a medium bowl, whisk together milk and eggs. Add milk mixture to flour mixture; stir just until moistened. Pour batter evenly into 7 greased 3 x 5½-inch loaf pans. Bake 20 to 25 minutes or until a toothpick inserted in center of bread comes out clean. Cool 10 minutes in pans. Remove from pans and serve warm or cool completely on a wire rack.

Yield: 7 mini loaves bread

43

Treat kids to cinnamony Popcorn Crunch Balls (clockwise from top left). Crispy Chicken Wings with Ranch-Style Dip are sure to be snatched up in a flash. Kissed with citrus flavor, Orange Cream Dip is wonderful served with fruit. Nutty Caramel Apple Snack Mix is munchably sweet.

CRISPY CHICKEN WINGS WITH RANCH-STYLE DIP

1	package (8 ounces) cream cheese, softened
1/2	cup sour cream
1	envelope (0.4 ounce) ranch-style salad dressing mix
2	pounds chicken wings
1	teaspoon salt
1 1/2	cups corn flake crumbs
3	egg whites

In a small bowl, combine cream cheese, sour cream, and salad dressing mix. Cover and chill until ready to serve.

Preheat oven to 375 degrees. Cut off and discard chicken wing tips. Cut chicken wings in half at joint. Sprinkle with salt; set aside. Place cereal crumbs and egg whites in separate small bowls. Beat egg whites until foamy. Dip chicken pieces, 1 at a time, in egg whites and roll in crumbs. Place on a greased baking sheet. Bake 30 to 40 minutes or until juices run clear when chicken is pierced with a fork. Serve warm with dip.
Yield: 18 to 22 pieces chicken

CARAMEL APPLE SNACK MIX

2 1/2	cups broken pretzel pieces
2 1/2	cups bite-size square rice cereal
2	cups apple-flavored round toasted oat cereal
1/2	cup sunflower kernels
1	package (14 ounces) caramels
1/4	cup water

Preheat oven to 250 degrees. In a large bowl, combine pretzels, rice cereal, oat cereal, and sunflower kernels. Place caramels and water in a small saucepan. Stirring frequently, cook over low heat until smooth. Pour caramel mixture over cereal mixture; stir until well coated. Spread mixture evenly in a greased 10 1/2 x 15 1/2-inch jellyroll pan. Bake 1 hour, stirring every 15 minutes. Spread on greased aluminum foil to cool. Break into pieces. Store in an airtight container.
Yield: about 10 cups snack mix

ORANGE CREAM DIP

1/2	cup sugar
1/4	cup orange juice
1	egg
2	tablespoons all-purpose flour
1	cup whipping cream, whipped
	Orange zest strip to garnish
	Fresh orange sections to serve

Combine sugar, orange juice, egg, and flour in a small saucepan. Whisking constantly, cook over medium-low heat about 12 minutes or until mixture thickens. Transfer to a medium bowl; cover and chill.

To serve, fold whipped cream into orange juice mixture. Garnish with orange zest. Serve with orange sections.
Yield: about 2 cups dip

POPCORN CRUNCH BALLS

8	cups popped popcorn
1/2	cup small red cinnamon candies
1	package (10 1/2 ounces) miniature marshmallows
3	tablespoons butter or margarine

Combine popcorn and candies in a large bowl. Place marshmallows and butter in a large saucepan. Stirring frequently, cook over low heat until marshmallows melt. Pour marshmallow mixture over popcorn mixture; stir until well coated. With greased hands, shape into 2 1/2-inch balls. Let popcorn cool completely. Store in an airtight container.
Yield: about 8 popcorn balls

GABRIEL'S HORNS

These sweet treats are best when eaten the day they are made.

- 2/3 cup purchased chocolate frosting
- 3 cups bugle-shaped corn snacks
- 6 ounces vanilla candy coating
  Multicolored non-pareils to decorate

Spoon frosting into a pastry bag fitted with a large round tip. Pipe frosting into each corn snack. In a small microwave-safe bowl, microwave candy coating on high power (100%) 2 minutes or until coating softens, stirring after 1 minute. Stir until smooth. Dip large end of each corn snack into candy coating. Sprinkle non-pareils over candy coating. Place on waxed paper; allow coating to harden. Cover with waxed paper (candies lose crispness if stored in a sealed container).
Yield: about 8 dozen snacks

CHOCOLATE-PEANUT BUTTER GRANOLA SQUARES

- 1 package (7 ounces) bran muffin mix
- 1/2 cup old-fashioned oats
- 1/4 cup firmly packed brown sugar
- 1/2 cup butter or margarine, softened
- 1/4 cup crunchy peanut butter
- 1/2 cup semisweet chocolate chips

Preheat oven to 325 degrees. In a medium bowl, combine muffin mix, oats, and brown sugar. With a pastry blender or 2 knives, cut in butter and peanut butter until mixture is well blended and crumbly. Stir in chocolate chips. Press into a 7 x 11-inch greased baking pan. Bake 28 to 32 minutes or until golden brown and firm. Cool in pan on a wire rack. Cut into 1 1/2-inch squares. Store in an airtight container.
Yield: about 2 dozen squares

Easy-to-make Gabriel's Horns (clockwise from top) *are playful party treats. Packed with chewy oats and brown sugar, Chocolate-Peanut Butter Granola Squares hit the spot when youngsters need an energy boost. Robust Bacon Cheese Dip is great served with veggies.*

BACON CHEESE DIP

- 8 ounces pasteurized process cheese
- 1 package (8 ounces) cream cheese
- 1/4 cup milk
- 1 tablespoon Worcestershire sauce
- 1 teaspoon onion powder
- 1/2 cup crumbled cooked bacon
  Carrot sticks to serve

In a medium saucepan, combine all ingredients except bacon. Stirring frequently, cook over low heat until smooth. Reserving 1 tablespoon bacon for garnish, stir in remaining bacon. Transfer to a serving container. Garnish with reserved bacon. Serve warm with carrot sticks.
Yield: about 2 1/4 cups dip

GINGERBREAD COOKIES

COOKIES

- 2/3 cup butter or margarine, softened
- 1/3 cup vegetable shortening
- 3/4 cup firmly packed brown sugar
- 1/2 cup buttermilk
- 1/2 cup molasses
- 2 eggs
- 1 teaspoon vanilla extract
- 5 1/4 cups all-purpose flour
- 1/4 cup cocoa
- 2 teaspoons ground cinnamon
- 1 1/2 teaspoons ground ginger
- 1 teaspoon ground allspice
- 1 teaspoon baking powder
- 1 teaspoon baking soda
- 1 teaspoon salt

ICING

- 1 1/2 cups confectioners sugar
- 5 teaspoons water
- 1/8 teaspoon icing whitener (used in cake decorating)
  Candies to decorate

For cookies, cream butter, shortening, and brown sugar in a large bowl until fluffy. Add buttermilk, molasses, eggs, and vanilla; beat until well blended. In another large bowl, combine remaining ingredients. Add half of dry ingredients to creamed mixture; stir until a soft dough forms. Stir in remaining dry ingredients, 1 cup at a time; use hands, if necessary, to mix well. Divide dough into fourths. Wrap in plastic wrap and chill 2 hours or until dough is firm.

Preheat oven to 350 degrees. On a lightly floured surface, use a floured rolling pin to roll out one fourth of dough to slightly less than 1/4-inch thickness. Use desired cookie cutters to cut out shapes. Transfer to a greased baking sheet. Bake 7 to 9 minutes or until firm. Transfer cookies to a wire rack to cool. Repeat with remaining dough.

For icing, combine all ingredients in a small bowl; stir until smooth. Spoon icing into a pastry bag fitted with a small round tip. Decorate cookies with icing and desired candies. Allow icing to harden. Store in an airtight container.

Yield: about 1 1/2 dozen 6-inch cookies or about 6 1/2 dozen 3 1/4-inch cookies

CHOCOLATE-TOFFEE BARS

- 1 package (18 ounces) refrigerated sugar cookie dough
- 1 cup almond brickle chips
- 1 cup semisweet chocolate chips
- 1/2 cup finely chopped pecans

Preheat oven to 350 degrees. Cut cookie dough into large pieces; press into bottom of a greased 9 x 13-inch baking pan. Sprinkle remaining ingredients evenly over dough. Bake 20 to 25 minutes or until edges are lightly browned. Cool in pan on a wire rack. Cut into 1 x 2-inch bars. Store in an airtight container.

Yield: about 4 dozen bars

PEANUT BUTTER HOT COCOA

- 9 cups milk, divided
- 1/2 cup smooth peanut butter
- 1 1/2 cups chocolate mix for milk
  Whipped cream to garnish

In a Dutch oven, combine 1 cup milk and peanut butter. Stirring frequently, cook over low heat until smooth. Increase heat to medium. Slowly stir in remaining 8 cups milk and chocolate mix. Stirring occasionally, cook just until mixture simmers. Garnish each serving with whipped cream; serve immediately.

Yield: about 9 1/2 cups cocoa

This year, have the kids host a holiday party! Children will have a ball decorating their own giant Gingerbread Cookies with icing and candies.

Peanut Butter Hot Cocoa is a tummy-warming treat, and Chocolate-Toffee Bars are soft and chewy.

Minty Marshmallow Fruit Dip (clockwise from left) *makes fresh apple slices extra yummy. Quick-and-easy Confetti Snack Mix is a mixture of store-bought goodies. Kids will love ooey, gooey S'More Chocolate Bars!*

S'MORE CHOCOLATE BARS

- 1 package (21.1 ounces) brownie mix
- 1/2 cup vegetable oil
- 1/2 cup water
- 1 egg
- 7 graham crackers (2 1/2 x 5-inch rectangles), coarsely crumbled
- 1 1/2 cups semisweet chocolate chips
- 3 cups miniature marshmallows

Preheat oven to 350 degrees. In a large bowl, combine brownie mix, oil, water, and egg; stir until well blended. Pour into a greased 9 x 13-inch baking pan. Sprinkle cracker crumbs over batter. Bake 20 minutes. Sprinkle chocolate chips over brownies; top with marshmallows. Bake 8 to 10 minutes longer or until marshmallows begin to brown. Cool in pan on a wire rack. Use an oiled knife to cut into 1 x 2-inch bars. Store in an airtight container.

Yield: about 4 dozen bars

MINTY MARSHMALLOW FRUIT DIP

- 1 package (8 ounces) cream cheese, softened
- 1 jar (7 ounces) marshmallow creme
- 1/4 cup finely crushed peppermint candies
  Crushed peppermint candies to garnish
  Apple slices to serve

In a medium bowl, beat cream cheese until fluffy. Add marshmallow creme; beat mixture until well blended. Stir in finely crushed peppermint candies. Store in an airtight container in refrigerator.

To serve, garnish dip with crushed peppermint candies. Serve with apple slices.

Yield: about 1 3/4 cups fruit dip

CONFETTI SNACK MIX

- 1 package (22 ounces) jelly beans
- 1 package (14 ounces) star-shaped milk chocolate candies
- 1 package (10 ounces) small peanut butter sandwich cookies
- 4 cups small pretzel twists
- 4 cups bite-size frosted wheat cereal

In a very large bowl, combine all ingredients. Store in an airtight container.

Yield: about 16 cups snack mix

Edible Necklaces

Children will have fun creating our clever cookie and candy necklaces! To fashion the edible party favors, we used a plastic needle to string gumdrops, wrapped peppermints, and candies with holes in the centers onto thin ribbon. Each necklace is completed by tying a cookie cutout to its center (a drinking straw is used to cut a hole in the top of each cookie before baking). The heart cookies are made using the Gingerbread Cookies recipe, page 46. What great goodies to wear home and eat later!

Small guests can create their own edible necklaces using their favorite candies and heart-shaped gingerbread cookies.

PEPPERMINT ICE CREAM PUNCH

1   jar (8 ounces) red maraschino cherries, drained
12 round peppermint candies
2   half-gallons vanilla ice cream, softened and divided
1   cup coarsely crushed peppermint candies (about 30 round candies), divided
48 ounces cherry lemon-lime soft drink, chilled

Place cherries and whole peppermint candies in bottom of a 6-cup ring mold. In a large bowl, combine 1 half-gallon ice cream and ¹/₂ cup crushed candies. Spoon ice cream mixture over cherries and candies in mold. Cover and freeze 4 hours or until firm.

In a large bowl, combine remaining half-gallon ice cream and ¹/₂ cup crushed candies; cover and store in freezer.

Surround a bowl of refreshing Peppermint Ice Cream Punch with a wreath of decorated gingerbread cookies. Spicy Baked Taco Dip is loaded with South-of-the-Border flavor, and Ham and Cheese Biscuit Turnovers make tasty appetizers!

To serve, spoon peppermint ice cream mixture into punch bowl. Stirring constantly, pour soft drink over ice cream mixture until blended. Dip mold into warm water to loosen ice cream ring. Place ice cream ring in punch.
Yield: about 16 cups punch

HAM AND CHEESE BISCUIT TURNOVERS

¹/₃ cup diced ham (about 3¹/₂ ounces)
¹/₃ cup shredded Cheddar cheese
2   tablespoons mayonnaise
1   can (7¹/₂ ounces) refrigerated buttermilk biscuits (10 count)

Preheat oven to 375 degrees. In a small bowl, combine ham, cheese, and mayonnaise. Press each biscuit into a 3-inch-diameter circle. Spoon about 1 tablespoon ham mixture in center of each biscuit and fold over; press edges together. Place on a greased baking sheet. Use scissors to cut slits in tops of turnovers. Bake 12 to 15 minutes or until golden brown. Serve warm.
Yield: 10 turnovers

BAKED TACO DIP

1   can (16 ounces) refried beans
¹/₂ teaspoon ground cumin
¹/₂ teaspoon garlic salt
¹/₂ teaspoon onion powder
¹/₂ pound lean ground beef
¹/₂ cup chopped onion
¹/₂ cup taco sauce
1¹/₂ cups (6 ounces) shredded Cheddar cheese
    Tortilla chips to serve

Preheat oven to 350 degrees. In a small bowl, combine beans, cumin, garlic salt, and onion powder. Spread mixture in bottom of a lightly greased 9-inch pie plate. In a small skillet, cook ground beef and onion over medium heat until meat is browned; drain well. Layer meat mixture, taco sauce, and cheese over bean mixture. Bake 25 to 30 minutes or until heated through and cheese is melted. Serve warm with chips.
Yield: about 3¹/₂ cups dip

Captivate little ones with a decorative Centerpiece House! Kids can decorate their own graham-cracker Cottages and ice-cream cone Trees with icing, candies, and other sweet treats.

CENTERPIECE HOUSE

This house is for decoration only.

You will need an empty 6½-inch-wide x 11-inch-long shoe box without a lid, cardboard, Royal Icing (recipe on page 53), craft knife, graham crackers

(2½ x 5 inches), coconut, pastry bag fitted with a large round tip, hot glue gun, and items to decorate house (we used gumdrops, hard candies, peppermint sticks, small red cinnamon

candies, butter-flavored cookies, and sugar wafer cookies).

1. To make front wall of house, draw a 6½-inch-wide x 5-inch-high rectangle on cardboard. Mark center top with a pencil. Refer to **Fig. 1** to draw a line 3 inches high from center mark and then to draw 2 connecting lines to form roof. Cut out shape. Repeat to make back wall. Place shoe box open side up. Glue pieces to each end of shoe box.

Fig. 1

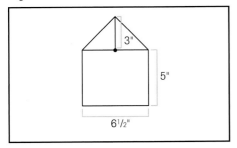

2. To make 1 side wall/roof piece of house, draw an 11-inch-wide by 9½-inch-high rectangle on cardboard. Cut out shape. Refer to **Fig. 2** to draw a line 5 inches from bottom. Use craft knife to score line. Bend cardboard to form roof. Repeat to make second side wall/roof piece. Glue pieces to each side of shoe box and along top of roof.

Fig. 2

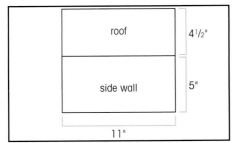

3. (**Note:** Use a serrated knife and a sawing motion to cut graham crackers.) Cut crackers as necessary to fit and hot glue to sides, front, and back of shoe box (do not glue graham crackers to roof).

4. Use pastry bag filled with royal icing to pipe windows onto sides of house and to attach door, shutters, cookies on roof, and candy decorations. Allow icing to harden.

COTTAGES AND TREES

For each cottage, you will need graham cracker halves (2½-inch square), Royal Icing (recipe on this page), white poster board, pastry bag, small and medium round tips, and items to decorate cottage (we used small red cinnamon candies,

gumdrops, stick gum, wrapped hard candies, small chocolate bars, and hard ring-shaped candies).

For each tree, you will need 1 cone-shaped sugar ice-cream cone, Royal Icing (recipe on this page) tinted green using green paste food coloring, and pastry bag fitted with medium tip.

1. (**Note:** Use a serrated knife and a sawing motion to cut graham crackers. Use royal icing and a medium tip to attach all cracker pieces and decorations to cottage.) Refer to **Fig. 1** to cut corners from 1 cracker half for front wall of cottage. Repeat for back wall.

Fig. 1

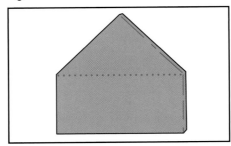

2. Refer to **Fig. 2** to attach front and back walls to 1 cracker half (base). Hold walls upright or use something to prop walls until icing hardens.

Fig. 2

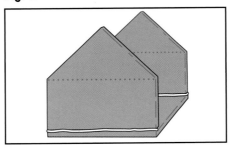

3. For side walls, refer to **Fig. 3** to attach 2 cracker quarters to base and front and back walls. Allow icing to harden.

Fig. 3

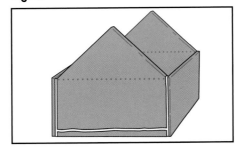

4. For roof, apply icing to top edges of walls. Refer to **Fig. 4** to place 2 cracker halves on top of cottage. Apply icing along peak of roof. Allow icing to harden.

Fig. 4

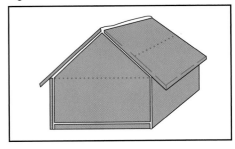

5. For yard, cut an irregularly shaped 6 x 7-inch piece from poster board. Use icing to attach cottage to poster board. Pipe snow onto roof.

6. Attach candies and other items to cottage for decorations. Decorate yard with sidewalk and shrubs.

7. Use small round tip to pipe icicles onto cottage and snow onto yard decorations. Allow icing to harden. Spread icing on poster board. Sprinkle yard with coconut; press into icing.

8. For tree, pipe swirls of green royal icing onto inverted ice-cream cones. Allow icing to harden.

ROYAL ICING

   5   cups confectioners sugar
   7   tablespoons warm water
   3   tablespoons plus 1 teaspoon meringue powder
  ½ teaspoon lemon extract

Beat confectioners sugar, water, meringue powder, and lemon extract in a medium bowl with an electric mixer 7 to 10 minutes or until stiff. Spoon icing into a pastry bag fitted with desired tip.

Yield: about 3¼ cups icing (will decorate centerpiece house **or** 5 cottages **or** 12 trees)

PRALINE PUMPKIN CHEESECAKE

CRUST
- 2/3 cup graham cracker crumbs
- 2/3 cup gingersnap cookie crumbs
- 2 tablespoons butter or margarine, melted

TOPPING
- 1 cup firmly packed brown sugar
- 6 tablespoons butter or margarine, softened
- 1 cup coarsely chopped pecans

FILLING
- 3 packages (8 ounces each) cream cheese, softened
- 1/2 cup granulated sugar
- 1/2 cup firmly packed brown sugar
- 1 can (15 ounces) pumpkin
- 4 eggs
- 1/4 cup evaporated milk
- 3 tablespoons all-purpose flour
- 2 tablespoons maple syrup
- 2 teaspoons pumpkin pie spice

For crust, combine cracker and cookie crumbs and butter in a small bowl. Press mixture into bottom of a lightly greased 10-inch springform pan.

For topping, combine brown sugar and butter in a small bowl. Stir in pecans.

Preheat oven to 325 degrees. For filling, beat cream cheese and sugars in a large bowl until fluffy. Beat in pumpkin, eggs, evaporated milk, flour, maple syrup, and pumpkin pie spice until smooth; pour over crust. With rack in center of oven, bake cake about 1 1/2 hours or until sides pull away from pan and center is almost set. Sprinkle topping over cake; bake 10 minutes longer. Leaving cake on same rack, broil 1 to 2 minutes or until sugar caramelizes and edges of cheesecake are golden brown. Cool in pan to room temperature on a wire rack. Remove sides of pan and serve.

Yield: about 16 servings

RASPBERRY-CHOCOLATE CAKE

CAKE
- 1 cup cocoa
- 2 cups boiling water
- 1 cup butter or margarine, softened
- 2 1/2 cups sugar
- 4 eggs
- 1 1/2 teaspoons vanilla extract
- 2 3/4 cups sifted all-purpose flour
- 2 teaspoons baking soda
- 1/2 teaspoon baking powder
- 1/2 teaspoon salt

FILLING
- 3 1/2 cups confectioners sugar
- 6 tablespoons butter or margarine, softened
- 6 tablespoons raspberry-flavored liqueur

ICING
- 1 package (6 ounces) semisweet chocolate chips
- 1 cup butter or margarine
- 1/2 cup half and half
- 2 1/2 cups confectioners sugar
- Gumdrop raspberry candies and silk leaves to garnish

For cake, grease and lightly flour three 9-inch round cake pans. In a medium bowl, combine cocoa and boiling water; whisk until smooth. Cool cocoa mixture completely.

Preheat oven to 350 degrees. In a large bowl, cream butter and sugar until fluffy. Add eggs and vanilla; beat until smooth. In a medium bowl, combine flour, baking soda, baking powder, and salt. Alternately beat dry ingredients and cocoa mixture into creamed mixture just until blended (do not overbeat). Pour batter into prepared pans. Bake 25 to 30 minutes or until a toothpick inserted in center of cake comes out clean. Cool in pans 10 minutes. Remove from pans and cool completely on a wire rack.

For filling, beat confectioners sugar, butter, and liqueur in a medium bowl until smooth and fluffy. Spread filling evenly between layers. Chill 2 hours.

For icing, combine chocolate chips, butter, and half and half in a medium saucepan over medium heat. Stirring constantly, cook about 6 to 8 minutes or until mixture is smooth. Remove from heat and whisk in confectioners sugar. Transfer icing to a medium bowl placed over a bowl of ice; beat about 8 minutes or until icing holds its shape. Spread icing on top and sides of cake, using back of a spoon to swirl icing. Store in an airtight container in refrigerator until ready to serve. To serve, garnish with candies and leaves.

Yield: about 16 servings

Rich Raspberry-Chocolate Cake (top) features a creamy filling kissed with fruit-flavored liqueur. Topped with a buttery brown sugar and pecan mixture, luscious Praline Pumpkin Cheesecake is an updated version of the traditional holiday pumpkin pie.

FESTIVE FAMILY FEASTS

*P*resent a festival of holiday fare to family and friends with a delightful array of delectable foods. Select an entire menu from our collection, or pick a handful of your favorite recipes and combine them for a most memorable meal. Ideal for Christmas or any time of the year, whatever feast you create is sure to be remembered by all!

Pork Tenderloin with Peach Chutney Glaze (recipe on page 58) is basted with a tangy, sweet mixture of preserves, raisins, and cider vinegar. Fresh sprigs of aromatic thyme and peach slices garnish this entrée with five-star flair.

A CHAMPAGNE CELEBRATION

MENU

Pineapple-Champagne Punch

Caviar on Toast

Roasted Red Pepper Dip

Cheesy Miniature Quiches

Wild Rice Salad

Pork Tenderloin with Peach Chutney Glaze

Marinated Onions and Olives

Scalloped Mushroom Potatoes

Tasty Pecan Muffins

Orange Curried Carrots

Lemon-Parsley Asparagus

Pumpkin Crème Brûlée

Shimmering Star Cookies

Bourbon-Pecan Cake

Holiday Coffee

PORK TENDERLOIN WITH PEACH CHUTNEY GLAZE (Shown on pages 56 and 57)

PEACH CHUTNEY
- 1 cup peach preserves
- 1/2 cup golden raisins
- 1/4 cup chopped pecans
- 2 tablespoons apple cider vinegar
- 2 teaspoons freshly grated ginger
- 1 teaspoon minced onion

PORK TENDERLOIN
- 1 tablespoon crushed fresh thyme leaves
- 2 cloves garlic, minced
- 2 teaspoons freshly grated ginger
- 1 teaspoon salt
- 1 teaspoon ground black pepper

- 1 pork tenderloin (about 2 pounds)
- Fresh thyme sprigs and canned peach slices to garnish

For peach chutney, process preserves, raisins, pecans, vinegar, ginger, and onion in a food processor until finely chopped. Transfer ingredients to a medium saucepan over low heat. Stirring frequently, cook 7 to 9 minutes or until mixture is heated through. Remove from heat. Cover and allow flavors to blend.

Preheat oven to 400 degrees. For pork tenderloin, combine thyme, garlic, ginger, salt, and pepper in a small bowl. Rub mixture over pork; place in a roasting pan. Insert meat thermometer into thickest portion of tenderloin. Spooning about 1/3 cup chutney over pork after 30 minutes, bake 40 to 50 minutes or until meat thermometer registers 160 degrees. Transfer tenderloin to a serving platter and allow to stand 10 minutes before slicing. Garnish with thyme sprigs and peach slices. Serve with remaining peach chutney.

Yield: about 10 servings

Toast the new year with Pineapple-Champagne Punch (clockwise from left), *a refreshing alternative to bottled bubbly. Fresh parsley and red caviar top an egg salad mixture for a festive appetizer in Caviar on Toast. For guests who have made slimming resolutions, robust Roasted Red Pepper Dip (recipe on page 60) is a low-fat treat they'll love "skinny dipping" into.*

PINEAPPLE-CHAMPAGNE PUNCH

Prepare ice ring and punch mixture the day before serving.

ICE RING
1 can (15¹/₄ ounces) pineapple tidbits in juice
1 can (11 ounces) mandarin oranges in light syrup
1 cup pineapple juice
1 jar (6 ounces) maraschino cherries, drained

PUNCH
2 cans (15¹/₄ ounces each) pineapple tidbits in juice
1¹/₂ cups orange-flavored liqueur
1¹/₂ cups sugar
1 cup pineapple juice
2 bottles (750 ml each) champagne, chilled

For ice ring, combine undrained pineapple, undrained oranges, pineapple juice, and cherries in an 8-cup ring mold. Cover and chill overnight.

For punch, combine undrained pineapple, liqueur, sugar, and pineapple juice in an airtight container. Stirring occasionally, cover and allow to stand overnight at room temperature. Chill mixture before serving.

To serve, place ice ring in bottom of a punch bowl. Pour punch mixture over ring. Slowly add chilled champagne; stir until blended. Serve immediately.

Yield: about nineteen 6-ounce servings

CAVIAR ON TOAST

6 hard-cooked eggs, well chilled
¹/₂ cup sour cream
2 tablespoons very finely chopped green onion
¹/₄ teaspoon salt
¹/₈ teaspoon ground white pepper
3¹/₂ tablespoons mayonnaise
3¹/₂ tablespoons butter, softened
2 loaves (16 ounces each) very thin-sliced white bread
1 jar (3¹/₂ ounces) red caviar, drained
³/₄ cup finely chopped fresh parsley

In a small bowl, finely shred eggs. Stir in sour cream, green onion, salt, and white pepper; cover and chill. In another small bowl, beat mayonnaise and butter until fluffy; cover and chill.

Continued on page 60

To serve, use a 3-inch star-shaped cookie cutter to cut a star from each slice of bread. Spread mayonnaise mixture over bread slices and transfer to a baking sheet. Toast bread under broiler until lightly browned. Place a heaping teaspoonful egg mixture in center of each toast. Place about ¼ teaspoon caviar in center of egg mixture. Press parsley onto sides of egg mixture. Serve immediately.
Yield: about 3 dozen appetizers

ROASTED RED PEPPER DIP
(Shown on page 59)

  2 large sweet red peppers
 ½ cup fat-free mayonnaise
 ½ cup fat-free sour cream
  1 tablespoon minced onion
  2 teaspoons chopped fresh
      parsley
  1 small clove garlic, minced
 ½ teaspoon white wine vinegar
 ¼ teaspoon ground white pepper
 ¼ teaspoon celery salt
 ¼ teaspoon salt
      Low-fat crackers to serve

To roast red peppers, cut in half lengthwise and remove seeds and membranes. Place skin side up on an ungreased baking sheet; use hand to flatten peppers. Broil about 3 inches from heat about 10 minutes or until peppers are blackened. Immediately seal peppers in a plastic bag and allow to steam 10 to 15 minutes. Remove charred skin and finely chop peppers.

In a medium bowl, combine chopped roasted red peppers, mayonnaise, sour cream, onion, parsley, garlic, vinegar, white pepper, celery salt, and salt. Stir until well blended. Cover and chill 1 hour to allow flavors to blend. Serve at room temperature with crackers.
Yield: about 2 cups dip

CHEESY MINIATURE QUICHES

  2 cups all-purpose flour
 ½ cup butter or margarine,
      melted

Baked in small tart pans, Cheesy Miniature Quiches are yummy morsels garnished with edible trims like carrot curls and sprigs of dill weed.

1½ teaspoons salt
 ¾ teaspoon ground red pepper
  4 cups (16 ounces) shredded
      sharp Cheddar cheese
  4 eggs
 ¾ cup milk
  8 ounces bacon, cooked and
      crumbled
 ½ cup frozen chopped spinach,
      thawed and squeezed dry
      Optional garnishes: cucumber
      slices, carrot curls, green
      onion brushes, red onion
      shreds, tomato peel, sweet
      red pepper, dill weed, celery
      leaves, celery slices, and
      green onion curls

Process flour, melted butter, salt, and red pepper in a food processor until combined. Add cheese; process until well blended. Shape dough into 1½-inch balls. Press dough into bottom and up sides of greased 2½-inch tart pans.

Preheat oven to 350 degrees. In a medium bowl, whisk eggs and milk. Stir in bacon and spinach. Spoon 1 tablespoon filling into each pastry shell. Bake 20 to 25 minutes or until center is set. Cool in pans 5 minutes. Remove from pans, garnish, and serve warm.
Yield: about 3 dozen quiches

WILD RICE SALAD

VINAIGRETTE

- 1 can (15¼ ounces) pineapple tidbits in juice
- ¼ cup rice wine vinegar
- 1 tablespoon dark sesame oil
- 1 tablespoon vegetable oil
- 1 tablespoon soy sauce
- 2 teaspoons sugar
- ¼ teaspoon ground red pepper

SALAD

- 2 cans (14½ ounces each) chicken broth
- 1 cup uncooked wild rice, rinsed
- 1 cup uncooked basmati rice
- 1½ cups shredded carrots (about 2 carrots)
- ½ cup golden raisins
- ½ cup sliced celery
- 2 tablespoons finely chopped green onion
  Carrot curls to garnish

For vinaigrette, drain pineapple, reserving juice. Set aside pineapple for salad. Combine reserved juice, vinegar, sesame oil, vegetable oil, soy sauce, sugar, and red pepper in a small bowl. Stir until well blended. Cover and let stand at room temperature to let flavors blend.

For salad, combine chicken broth and wild rice in a heavy large saucepan. Bring to a boil over medium-high heat. Stir rice and cover; reduce heat to low and simmer about 30 minutes. Stir in basmati rice and continue to simmer about 20 minutes or until rice is tender. Transfer rice to a 2½-quart serving bowl and allow to cool. Stir after 15 minutes.

Add reserved pineapple, carrots, raisins, celery, and green onion to rice; lightly toss. Pour vinaigrette over salad and lightly toss until salad is coated. Garnish with carrot curls. Serve at room temperature.

Yield: about 11 cups salad

Wild Rice Salad is a flavorful medley of rice, pineapple, raisins, and carrots tossed in a zesty vinaigrette just before serving.

TASTY PECAN MUFFINS

1 cup all-purpose flour
3/4 cup whole-wheat flour
3 tablespoons sugar
2 teaspoons baking powder
1 teaspoon salt
1 cup milk
2 eggs
1/2 cup butter or margarine, melted
2/3 cup chopped pecans, toasted
and coarsely ground

Preheat oven to 350 degrees. In a medium bowl, combine flours, sugar, baking powder, and salt. Make a well in center of dry ingredients. In a small bowl, combine milk, eggs, and melted butter; beat until well blended. Add to dry ingredients; stir until well blended. Stir in pecans. Fill greased muffin cups about two-thirds full. Bake 25 to 28 minutes or until a toothpick inserted in center of muffin comes out clean and edges of muffins are lightly browned. Cool in pan 5 minutes. Serve warm or cool completely.
Yield: about 1 dozen muffins

MARINATED ONIONS AND OLIVES

1/4 cup olive oil
2 tablespoons freshly squeezed lime juice (about 1 lime)
2 tablespoons white wine vinegar
2 cloves garlic, minced
1 teaspoon dried red pepper flakes
1 teaspoon cumin seed
1 can (6 ounces) small pitted ripe olives, drained
2 jars (3 ounces each) pimiento-stuffed green olives, drained
1 jar (3 ounces) almond-stuffed green olives, drained
2 jars (3 ounces each) cocktail onions, drained
3 tablespoons chopped fresh cilantro

Combine olive oil, lime juice, vinegar, garlic, red pepper flakes, and cumin seed in a medium saucepan. Bring to a boil over medium-high heat. Remove from heat and allow to cool. Stir in olives, onions, and cilantro. Transfer mixture to an airtight container. Chill overnight to allow

Marinated Onions and Olives (clockwise from top) *will add zing to your holiday relish tray. Tasty Pecan Muffins are packed with toasted nuts and hearty whole grain goodness. A crunchy cracker crumb topping adds flavorful texture to cheesy Scalloped Mushroom Potatoes.*

flavors to blend. Serve at room temperature.
Yield: about 4 cups olives

SCALLOPED MUSHROOM POTATOES

6 medium unpeeled potatoes
1 1/2 teaspoons salt, divided
1 cup finely chopped onion
1 clove garlic, minced
1/4 cup butter or margarine
1 can (10 3/4 ounces) golden mushroom soup
1 container (8 ounces) sour cream
1/4 teaspoon ground black pepper
8 ounces fresh mushrooms, sliced
1 sweet red pepper, cut into thin rings
3/4 cup coarsely crushed poppy seed crackers
2 tablespoons butter or margarine, melted
1/2 cup shredded Monterey Jack cheese

In a heavy large saucepan, cover potatoes with water and add 1 teaspoon salt. Bring to a boil over medium-high heat. Reduce heat to medium. Cover and cook about 30 minutes or until potatoes are tender. Remove from heat, drain, and cool.

In a heavy medium skillet, sauté onion and garlic in 1/4 cup butter over medium heat until tender. Stir in soup, sour cream, remaining 1/2 teaspoon salt, and black pepper until mixture is well blended. Remove from heat.

Preheat oven to 350 degrees. Peel potatoes and cut into thin slices. Place half of potato slices in a greased 9 x 13-inch baking dish. Place half of mushroom slices over potatoes. Spoon half of soup mixture over vegetables. Layer remaining potatoes, mushrooms, and soup mixture. Place pepper rings over casserole.

In a small bowl, combine cracker crumbs and melted butter. Stir in cheese. Sprinkle mixture over casserole. Bake 30 to 35 minutes or until casserole is hot and bubbly. Serve warm.
Yield: about 12 servings

Covered with a creamy sauce, Orange Curried Carrots (top) are spicy and delicious. A buttery blend of lemon zest, sautéed onions, and sesame seed gives Lemon-Parsley Asparagus its unique flavor.

ORANGE CURRIED CARROTS

2 pounds carrots, peeled and sliced
1 can (11 ounces) mandarin oranges in light syrup, divided
1½ teaspoons salt, divided
½ teaspoon ground white pepper, divided
2 tablespoons butter or margarine
1 tablespoon finely minced onion
2 tablespoons all-purpose flour
1½ teaspoons curry powder
1½ cups warm milk
¼ teaspoon ground cinnamon
⅛ teaspoon ground ginger

Place carrots in a microwave-safe serving dish. Drain oranges, reserving syrup. Pour ¼ cup reserved mandarin orange syrup over carrots. Sprinkle ½ teaspoon salt and ¼ teaspoon white pepper over carrots. Cover and microwave on high power (100%) 8 to 12 minutes or until carrots are tender, stirring halfway through cooking. Keep carrots covered while preparing sauce.

Reserve a few orange segments for garnish and chop remaining oranges into pieces. Melt butter in a heavy medium saucepan over medium heat. Sauté onion in butter until tender. Sprinkle flour and curry powder over butter. Stirring constantly, cook until mixture is well blended and thickened. Gradually add remaining reserved orange syrup and milk; stir until well blended. Stirring constantly, add chopped oranges, remaining 1 teaspoon salt, remaining ¼ teaspoon white pepper, cinnamon, and ginger. Cook about 15 minutes or until sauce thickens. Drain carrots; pour sauce over carrots. Garnish with reserved orange segments. Serve warm.
Yield: about 10 servings

LEMON-PARSLEY ASPARAGUS

½ cup butter, divided
1 tablespoon sesame seed
1 tablespoon finely minced onion
2 tablespoons chopped fresh parsley
2 tablespoons freshly squeezed lemon juice
½ teaspoon grated lemon zest
½ teaspoon salt
¼ teaspoon ground black pepper
4 cans (15 ounces each) asparagus spears, drained
Lemon zest strips and fresh parsley to garnish

In a medium skillet, combine 2 tablespoons butter, sesame seed, and onion over medium heat. Stirring frequently, cook until sesame seed is lightly browned and onion is tender. Add remaining 6 tablespoons butter, stirring constantly until butter melts. Remove from heat and stir in chopped parsley, lemon juice, lemon zest, salt, and pepper.

Place asparagus in a microwave-safe serving dish. Cover and microwave on high power (100%) 3 to 5 minutes or until heated through, rotating dish halfway through cooking time. Pour butter mixture over asparagus. Garnish with lemon zest strips and parsley. Serve warm.
Yield: 8 to 10 servings

PUMPKIN CRÈME BRÛLÉE

2½ cups milk
½ cup granulated sugar
2 tablespoons maple syrup
3 eggs
2 egg yolks
1 cup canned pumpkin
1 teaspoon vanilla extract
½ teaspoon ground cinnamon
¼ teaspoon ground ginger
¼ teaspoon ground nutmeg
⅛ teaspoon ground cloves
½ cup firmly packed brown sugar

Preheat oven to 325 degrees. Grease eight 6-ounce ramekins. In a heavy large saucepan, combine milk, granulated sugar, and maple syrup over medium-low heat. Stirring frequently, cook about 8 minutes or until sugar dissolves. Remove from heat. In a large bowl, beat whole eggs and egg yolks. Add pumpkin, vanilla, cinnamon, ginger, nutmeg, and cloves; beat until well blended. Slowly beat in warm milk mixture. Pour custard mixture into prepared ramekins. Place ramekins in a roasting pan. Add hot water to roasting pan to come halfway up sides of ramekins. Bake 55 to 60 minutes or until a knife inserted near center of custard comes out clean. Remove ramekins from roasting pan and allow to cool. Cover and chill overnight.

To serve, sprinkle 1 tablespoon brown sugar over each chilled custard. Place ramekins on a baking sheet and broil 4 inches from heat about 2 to 3 minutes or until sugar caramelizes. Serve immediately.
Yield: 8 servings

SHIMMERING STAR COOKIES

COOKIES
¾ cup butter or margarine, softened
½ cup sugar
1 egg
¾ teaspoon almond extract
1¾ cups all-purpose flour

Pumpkin Crème Brûlée (top) *is a dreamy creation baked in ramekins. Icing and glitter transform simple sugar cookies into elegant dessert fare in Shimmering Star Cookies.*

3 tablespoons cornstarch
½ teaspoon baking powder
⅛ teaspoon salt

ICING
1½ cups confectioners sugar
2 tablespoons plus 1 teaspoon milk
¼ teaspoon almond extract
White edible glitter to decorate

Preheat oven to 350 degrees. For cookies, cream butter and sugar in a medium bowl until fluffy. Add egg and almond extract; beat until smooth. In a small bowl, combine flour, cornstarch, baking powder, and salt. Add dry ingredients to creamed mixture; stir until a soft dough forms. On a lightly floured surface, use a floured rolling pin to roll out dough to ⅛-inch thickness. Use a 2-inch star-shaped cookie cutter to cut out cookies. Transfer to a greased baking sheet. Bake 5 to 7 minutes or until bottoms of cookies are lightly browned. Transfer to a wire rack with waxed paper underneath to cool completely.

For icing, combine confectioners sugar, milk, and almond extract in a medium bowl; stir until smooth. Spoon a small amount of icing in center of 1 cookie; top with a second cookie, offsetting points of stars. Place on wire rack. Repeat with remaining pairs of cookies. Drizzle icing over cookies. While icing is wet, sprinkle with glitter. Allow icing to harden.
Yield: about 4 dozen stacked cookies

Drenched with a spirited glaze, moist Bourbon-Pecan Cake is the perfect finale to the night's festivities. For a flavorful, aromatic beverage, try Holiday Coffee kissed with cinnamon, cloves, and vanilla.

BOURBON-PECAN CAKE

CAKE
- 1 package (18½ ounces) butter cake mix
- 1 package (3.4 ounces) vanilla instant pudding mix
- 4 eggs
- ¾ cup water
- ½ cup vegetable oil
- ¼ cup bourbon
- 1 cup chopped pecans

GLAZE
- 1 cup sugar
- ½ cup butter or margarine
- ¼ cup water
- ¼ cup bourbon

Preheat oven to 325 degrees. For cake, combine cake and pudding mixes in a large bowl. Add eggs, water, oil, and bourbon; beat 2 minutes or until well blended. Stir in pecans. Pour batter into a greased 10-inch fluted tube pan. Bake 55 to 60 minutes or until a toothpick inserted in center of cake comes out clean. Place pan on a wire rack to cool 10 minutes. Invert onto a serving plate.

For glaze, combine sugar, butter, and water in a medium saucepan over medium-high heat; bring to a boil. Reduce heat to medium; stirring constantly, cook 2 to 3 minutes. Remove from heat; stir in bourbon. Pour hot glaze over warm cake. Allow cake to cool completely.
Yield: about 16 servings

HOLIDAY COFFEE

- ⅓ cup ground coffee
- 2 cinnamon sticks, broken into pieces
- 6 whole cloves
- 1 vanilla bean (about 3 inches long)
- 1½ quarts water

Combine coffee, cinnamon pieces, and cloves in an airtight container. Split vanilla bean and scrape seeds into mixture. Cut vanilla bean into 3 pieces and add to mixture. Cover and store in an airtight container overnight to allow flavors to blend.

To serve, brew coffee mixture and water in a 10-cup coffee maker. Serve hot.
Yield: about eight 6-ounce servings

BOUNTIFUL BUFFET

MENU

Cherry Salad Mold	Oyster Dressing
Cream of Spinach Soup	Creamed Fennel and Leeks
Lemon Pepper-Parmesan Crackers	Acorn Squash Rings
Orange-Peach Gelatin Salad	Cranberry-Pineapple Chutney
Green Autumn Salad with Orange Vinaigrette	Corn Soufflé
Golden Whole-Wheat Rolls	Cinnamon Cider
Glazed Roast Turkey with Horseradish Sauce	Indian Pudding
Apple and Vegetable Sauté	Pumpkin Spice Cake

GLAZED ROAST TURKEY WITH HORSERADISH SAUCE

GLAZED TURKEY

1 1/2 cups apple jelly
1/2 cup balsamic vinegar
1 tablespoon grated lemon zest
2 teaspoons salt
1 1/2 teaspoons ground black pepper
1 turkey (13 to 15 pounds)
    Salt and ground black pepper
1 cup water

HORSERADISH SAUCE

2 tablespoons butter or margarine
3/4 cup minced onion
2 tablespoons all-purpose flour
1/2 cup chicken broth
3/4 cup apple jelly
1 jar (5 ounces) cream-style
    prepared horseradish
1/2 teaspoon salt
1/8 teaspoon ground white pepper
1/2 cup whipping cream

For glazed turkey, combine jelly, vinegar, lemon zest, 2 teaspoons salt, and 1 1/2 teaspoons pepper in a small saucepan. Stirring frequently, cook over medium heat until jelly melts. Remove glaze from heat.

Preheat oven to 350 degrees. Remove giblets and neck from turkey; reserve for Oyster Dressing (recipe on page 68). Rinse turkey and pat dry. Salt and pepper inside of turkey. Tie ends of legs to tail with kitchen twine. Place turkey, breast side up, in a large roasting pan. Insert meat thermometer into thickest part of thigh, making sure thermometer does not touch bone. Pour water into pan. Baste

Roasted until succulent and golden brown, Glazed Roast Turkey will have guests coming back for more, especially when served with savory Horseradish Sauce. Sweet apple slices, turnips, carrots, and onions are combined for Apple and Vegetable Sauté. A colorful accompaniment to the entrée, Cherry Salad Mold (not shown) is creamy and delicious.

turkey with glaze. Loosely cover with aluminum foil. Basting with glaze every 30 minutes, roast 3 to 3 1/2 hours or until meat thermometer registers 180 degrees and juices run clear when thickest part of thigh is pierced with a fork. Remove foil during last hour to allow turkey to brown. Transfer turkey to a serving platter and let stand 20 minutes before carving.

For horseradish sauce, melt butter in a heavy medium saucepan over medium heat. Add onion and sauté about 6 minutes or until transparent. Stirring constantly, add flour and cook 3 minutes or until mixture is bubbly. Stir in chicken broth; continue to stir until thick and well blended. Stir in jelly, horseradish, salt, and white pepper; cook until jelly melts. Gradually stir in whipping cream and bring to a simmer. Serve warm sauce with turkey.
Yield: 15 to 18 servings

APPLE AND VEGETABLE SAUTÉ

1/2 cup butter or margarine
5 medium unpeeled turnips, quartered
4 medium carrots, cut into 2-inch-long pieces
3 medium onions, quartered with root ends intact
1 cup firmly packed brown sugar
2 unpeeled Granny Smith apples, cored and cut into eighths
2 unpeeled Rome apples, cored and cut into eighths
1 tablespoon balsamic vinegar
1/2 teaspoon salt
1/2 teaspoon ground black pepper

Melt butter in a 12-inch-diameter x 2 1/2-inch-deep heavy skillet over medium-high heat. Add turnips to butter; sauté about 5 minutes. Add carrots and onions; cook on 1 side about 10 minutes or until golden brown. Carefully turn vegetables over and brown other side. Sprinkle brown sugar over mixture. Reduce heat to medium; continue to cook about

20 minutes or until vegetables are almost tender. Add apples to vegetables. Cook mixture about 7 to 10 minutes or until apples are completely browned and tender, carefully turning as necessary. Add vinegar, salt, and pepper; toss lightly. Serve immediately.
Yield: 8 to 10 servings

CHERRY SALAD MOLD

1 package (3 ounces) cherry gelatin
1 package (3 ounces) raspberry gelatin
2 cups boiling water
2 packages (8 ounces each) cream cheese, softened
1 can (10 3/4 ounces) crushed pineapple, drained
2 cans (16 ounces each) pitted bing cherries, drained with juice reserved
1 cup miniature marshmallows
1/2 cup chopped pecans

In a large bowl, dissolve gelatins in boiling water. Add cream cheese and beat until smooth. Stir in fruit, marshmallows, pecans, and 1/2 cup reserved cherry juice. Pour into a lightly oiled 8-cup gelatin mold. Cover and chill until firm.
Yield: 10 to 12 servings

OYSTER DRESSING

- 4 cups water
  Giblets and neck from turkey
- 1 cup chopped onion
- 1 cup chopped celery
- 1/2 cup butter or margarine
- 3/4 cup sliced fresh mushrooms
- 7 cups corn bread crumbs
- 1/4 cup chopped fresh parsley
- 2 teaspoons poultry seasoning
- 2 teaspoons rubbed sage
- 1 teaspoon salt
- 2 containers (10 ounces each) fresh oysters, drained and chopped
- 2 eggs, beaten

Place water, giblets, and neck in a medium saucepan; bring to a boil over medium heat. Cover, reduce heat, and simmer 1 hour or until meat is tender. Reserve broth and chop meat.

Preheat oven to 350 degrees. In a medium skillet, sauté onion and celery in butter over medium heat. When vegetables are almost tender, add mushrooms; cook 2 minutes and remove from heat. In a large bowl, combine crumbs, parsley, poultry seasoning, sage, salt, meat, and vegetables. Stir in oysters, eggs, and 2 cups giblet broth, adding additional broth as necessary to moisten. Spoon into a greased 9 x 13-inch baking dish. Cover and bake 45 minutes. Uncover and bake 15 to 20 minutes or until lightly browned. Serve warm.
Yield: 12 to 14 servings

LEMON PEPPER-PARMESAN CRACKERS

- 2 cups all-purpose flour
- 1 cup grated Parmesan cheese
- 1 tablespoon dried parsley flakes
- 2 teaspoons lemon pepper
- 1 small clove garlic, minced
- 1 cup chilled butter, cut into pieces

In a medium bowl, combine flour, cheese, parsley, lemon pepper, and garlic until well blended. Using a pastry blender or 2 knives, cut in butter

Corn bread dressing, a Southern great, is given an Eastern Seaboard flavor with fresh shellfish. Moist Oyster Dressing is packed with the flavorful taste of sage and other seasonings.

until mixture resembles coarse meal. Shape dough into a ball; wrap in plastic wrap and chill 30 minutes.

Preheat oven to 350 degrees. On a lightly floured surface, use a floured rolling pin to roll out dough to 1/4-inch thickness. Cut out crackers with a

3 x 2 1/2-inch leaf-shaped cookie cutter. Transfer to an ungreased baking sheet and bake 15 to 20 minutes or until golden brown. Serve warm or cool completely on a wire rack.
Yield: about 2 1/2 dozen crackers

Rich, delicious Cream of Spinach Soup is an inviting start to your holiday meal. Cut in leaf shapes, Lemon Pepper-Parmesan Crackers are melt-in-your-mouth good!

CREAM OF SPINACH SOUP

1 1/2 cups finely chopped onions
1/4 cup butter or margarine
2 cloves garlic, minced
3 tablespoons all-purpose flour
3/4 teaspoon salt
1/4 teaspoon ground black pepper
3 cups chicken broth
2 pounds fresh spinach, washed, stemmed, and drained
1 medium potato, chopped
1 medium carrot, sliced
1 cup half and half
Bacon pieces and carrot strips to garnish

In a Dutch oven, sauté onions in butter over medium heat until soft. Add garlic; sauté 2 to 3 minutes. Stirring constantly, add flour, salt, and pepper; cook about 3 minutes or until mixture is well blended. Gradually stir in chicken broth. Increase heat to medium high and add spinach, potato, and carrot; bring mixture to a boil. Reduce heat to medium low, cover, and cook until vegetables are tender. Process soup in a food processor until vegetables are finely chopped; return to Dutch oven over medium-low heat. Stirring constantly, gradually add half and half; simmer until heated through. Garnish each serving with bacon and carrot strips.
Yield: about 8 cups soup

ORANGE-PEACH GELATIN SALAD

- 2 cups boiling water
- 1 package (6 ounces) orange gelatin
- 3/4 cup cold water
- 2 containers (8 ounces each) peach yogurt
- 1 can (16 ounces) peach slices, drained
- 1 can (11 ounces) mandarin oranges, drained

In a medium bowl, stir boiling water into gelatin until gelatin dissolves. For top gelatin layer, place 1/2 cup gelatin mixture in a small bowl and stir in cold water. Cover and set aside; do not refrigerate. Stir yogurt into remaining 1 1/2 cups gelatin mixture. Pour yogurt mixture into a 2 1/2-quart serving dish; chill until firm.

Arrange peach and orange slices in a swirled pattern on top of chilled yogurt mixture. Carefully pour reserved gelatin mixture over fruit slices. Chill until firm.

Yield: about 10 servings

Tangy Orange-Peach Gelatin Salad (top left) is bursting with luscious fruit. Hearty Golden Whole-Wheat Rolls are yummy served toasty warm. Green Autumn Salad with Orange Vinaigrette is a colorful medley of mixed greens, avocados, grapes, artichoke hearts, and red onion tossed with a zippy dressing.

GREEN AUTUMN SALAD WITH ORANGE VINAIGRETTE

ORANGE VINAIGRETTE

- 1/4 cup sugar
- 1 teaspoon dry mustard
- 1 teaspoon paprika
- 1/2 teaspoon salt
- 1/4 cup freshly squeezed orange juice
- 3 tablespoons white vinegar
- 1 teaspoon minced onion
- 1 teaspoon grated orange zest
- 3/4 cup vegetable oil

SALAD

- 12 to 14 cups mixed salad greens (we used arugula, radicchio, and red leaf lettuce)
- 2 medium avocados, peeled, pitted, and sliced
- 1 1/2 cups red seedless grapes
- 1 jar (6 ounces) marinated artichoke hearts, drained and chopped
- 1 small red onion, sliced and separated into rings
- 1 rib celery, chopped
- 4 teaspoons sesame seed, toasted

For orange vinaigrette, combine sugar, dry mustard, paprika, and salt in a blender or food processor. Add orange juice, vinegar, onion, and orange zest to dry ingredients; blend until well mixed. With blender running, slowly pour oil into orange juice mixture. Transfer vinaigrette to an airtight container. Chill until ready to serve.

For salad, combine salad greens, avocado slices, grapes, artichoke pieces, onion rings, and celery in a large bowl. To serve, pour orange vinaigrette over salad and gently toss. Sprinkle with toasted sesame seed. Serve immediately.

Yield: about 12 servings

GOLDEN WHOLE-WHEAT ROLLS

- 3/4 cup milk
- 3/4 cup water
- 1/3 cup butter or margarine
- 1/3 cup honey
- 2 packages dry yeast
- 2 3/4 cups whole-wheat flour, divided
- 2 3/4 cups all-purpose flour, divided
- 1/2 cup yellow cornmeal
- 1 1/2 teaspoons salt
- 3 eggs, beaten
  Vegetable cooking spray
- 1 egg, beaten

Combine milk, water, and butter in a small saucepan. Stir over medium heat until butter melts; stir in honey. Remove from heat and allow liquid mixture to cool to 110 degrees. Add yeast; stir until dissolved. In a large bowl, combine 2 1/2 cups whole-wheat flour, 2 1/2 cups all-purpose flour, cornmeal, and salt. Add yeast mixture and 3 beaten eggs to flour mixture; stir until a soft dough forms. Turn dough onto a lightly floured surface. Knead 6 to 10 minutes or until dough becomes smooth and elastic, using additional flour as necessary. Place in a large bowl sprayed with cooking spray, turning once to coat top of dough. Cover and let rise in a warm place (80 to 85 degrees) 1 hour or until doubled in size.

Turn dough onto a lightly floured surface and punch down. Shape dough into 24 balls and divide between two greased 9-inch round cake pans. Spray tops of rolls with cooking spray, cover, and let rise in a warm place 1 hour or until doubled in size.

Preheat oven to 400 degrees. Brush rolls with remaining beaten egg. Bake 12 to 15 minutes or until golden brown. Serve warm or transfer to a wire rack to cool completely.

Yield: 2 dozen rolls

CREAMED FENNEL AND LEEKS

2 fennel bulbs (about 1½ pounds)
4 leeks
3 tablespoons olive oil
2 cloves garlic, finely chopped
½ teaspoon dried dill weed
½ teaspoon salt
1 cup whipping cream
1 cup milk
¼ cup butter or margarine
3 tablespoons all-purpose flour
¾ teaspoon salt
¼ teaspoon ground black pepper
¼ cup shredded Parmesan cheese

Cut off fennel stalks, reserving some of the feathery leaves for garnish. Quarter fennel bulbs and core; thinly slice to yield about 3¼ cups. Thinly slice leeks, using only white and pale green portions, to yield about 5½ cups. In a large skillet over medium heat, sauté leeks in hot oil 3 minutes. Cover and cook about 2 minutes or until leeks begin to wilt. Add fennel, garlic, dill weed, and salt; sauté about 5 to 7 minutes or until vegetables are tender (fennel will remain slightly crisp). Cover and remove from heat.

Combine whipping cream and milk in a small microwave-safe bowl. Microwave on high power (100%) 3 minutes or until liquid begins to simmer. Melt butter in a large saucepan over medium heat. Whisking constantly, add flour, salt, and pepper; cook until very lightly browned and thickened. Slowly add hot cream mixture; whisk constantly until smooth and thick. Reduce heat to medium low. Whisking frequently, simmer about 3 to 5 minutes or until mixture reduces in volume. Add vegetables to sauce. Reduce heat to low; cover and simmer about 5 minutes or until heated through.

Preheat broiler. Pour mixture into a 9-inch square baking dish. Sprinkle cheese over top. Broil about 2 minutes or until top is golden brown. Garnish with reserved fennel leaves. Serve warm.

Yield: about 8 servings

Creamed Fennel and Leeks (left) *is seasoned with a hint of dill. Another great dish that goes well with our roast turkey, Acorn Squash Rings have a fanciful shape and delicate maple flavor.*

ACORN SQUASH RINGS

3 unpeeled acorn squash
¼ cup butter or margarine, melted
½ cup maple syrup
¼ cup firmly packed brown sugar
1½ teaspoons ground cardamom

Preheat oven to 375 degrees. Cut each squash in half crosswise and remove seeds. Place squash, cut side down, in a 10½ x 15½ x 1-inch jellyroll pan; pour water into pan to a depth of ½ inch. Bake 20 minutes. Remove from oven and allow to cool enough to handle.

Cut squash crosswise into ½-inch rings; discard ends. Place rings in 2 greased jellyroll pans. Brush butter onto both sides of squash rings; drizzle with maple syrup. Combine brown sugar and cardamom in a small bowl; sprinkle mixture over squash. Cover pans with aluminum foil and bake 25 minutes. Remove foil and turn each slice. Bake uncovered 20 minutes or until squash is tender, alternating position of pans in oven once during baking. Serve warm.

Yield: about 8 servings

CRANBERRY-PINEAPPLE CHUTNEY

2 teaspoons pickling spice
1 package (12 ounces) fresh cranberries
2 cups firmly packed brown sugar
1 can (15¼ ounces) pineapple tidbits in juice
1½ cups golden raisins
½ cup apple cider vinegar
½ cup finely chopped onion
1 tablespoon grated orange zest

Place pickling spice in a small cheesecloth square and tie with kitchen string. Combine cranberries, brown sugar, undrained pineapple, raisins, vinegar, onion, and orange zest in a heavy Dutch oven over medium-high heat. Place spice bag in mixture. Stirring frequently, cook about 25 to 35 minutes or until cranberries are tender and mixture thickens. Remove from heat and allow to cool. Remove spice bag. Serve at room temperature.

Yield: about 4½ cups chutney

Sweet, tart Cranberry-Pineapple Chutney (left) is a refreshing change from traditional cranberry sauce. For a touch of gourmet cooking, light and fluffy Corn Soufflé is a dish that everyone will love.

CORN SOUFFLÉ

¼ cup butter or margarine
2 tablespoons finely chopped onion
2 tablespoons finely chopped sweet red pepper
2 tablespoons finely chopped sweet yellow pepper
¼ cup all-purpose flour
1 teaspoon curry powder
1 cup milk
4 eggs, separated
1 package (10 ounces) frozen whole kernel yellow corn, thawed
1 teaspoon salt
⅛ teaspoon ground black pepper
2 tablespoons grated Parmesan cheese

Preheat oven to 350 degrees. In a heavy medium saucepan, melt butter over medium heat; add onion and red and yellow peppers and sauté about 5 minutes or until vegetables are tender. Gradually stir in flour and curry powder until well blended. Add milk, whisking about 2 minutes or until mixture is thick and smooth; remove from heat. In a small bowl, slightly beat egg yolks. Stirring constantly, add a small amount of hot mixture to egg yolks; stir egg mixture back into hot mixture in saucepan. Stir in corn, salt, and black pepper. In a medium bowl, beat egg whites until stiff peaks form. Fold in egg whites. Sprinkle cheese over bottom and sides of a buttered 1½-quart soufflé dish. Spoon corn mixture into dish. Bake 45 to 50 minutes or until soufflé is set. Serve immediately.
Yield: 6 to 8 servings

INDIAN PUDDING

    3   cups milk
  1/2   cup yellow cornmeal
    2   eggs
  1/3   cup molasses
  1/4   cup firmly packed brown sugar
    2   tablespoons butter or margarine
  3/4   teaspoon ground cinnamon
  1/4   teaspoon ground ginger
  1/4   teaspoon baking soda
  1/8   teaspoon salt
        Whipping cream to serve

Preheat oven to 325 degrees. Scald milk in a large saucepan over medium heat. Reduce heat to low and slowly whisk in cornmeal. Whisking frequently, cook about 5 minutes or until mixture thickens. Remove from heat. In a small bowl, beat eggs. Slowly whisk 1 cup cornmeal mixture into beaten eggs; gradually stir egg mixture back into hot cornmeal in saucepan. Add molasses, brown sugar, butter, cinnamon, ginger, baking soda, and salt; stir until well blended. Pour into a greased 2-quart baking dish. Bake 1 to 1 1/4 hours or until sides are set but center is still soft. Serve warm with whipping cream.
Yield: about 8 servings

CINNAMON CIDER

   48   ounces apple cider
  2/3   cup water
  1/3   cup granulated sugar
    2   tablespoons firmly packed
          brown sugar
    1   teaspoon ground cinnamon
  1/4   teaspoon ground nutmeg
  2/3   cup cinnamon schnapps
    2   tablespoons freshly squeezed
          lemon juice
        Lemon slices to garnish

Combine apple cider, water, sugars, cinnamon, and nutmeg in a Dutch oven over medium-high heat; stir until sugars dissolve. Bring mixture to a boil. Reduce heat to low. Add schnapps and lemon juice; heat thoroughly. Garnish each serving with a lemon slice.
Yield: about nine 6-ounce servings

An original New England favorite, Indian Pudding is a custard-like concoction of cornmeal, molasses, brown sugar, and spices that's served warm with a drizzling of cream. A cup of spirited Cinnamon Cider garnished with a lemon slice is the perfect accompaniment.

A thick, buttery icing kissed with maple syrup crowns moist Pumpkin Spice Cake. It'll be hard to resist sampling this scrumptious dessert.

PUMPKIN SPICE CAKE

CAKE
- 3/4 cup butter or margarine, softened
- 2 cups sugar
- 1 can (15 ounces) pumpkin
- 4 eggs
- 1 teaspoon vanilla extract
- 3 cups all-purpose flour
- 2 1/2 teaspoons ground cinnamon
- 2 teaspoons baking soda
- 1 1/2 teaspoons ground cloves
- 1/2 teaspoon salt
- 1 cup chopped walnuts
- 1 cup raisins

ICING
- 1/2 cup butter or margarine
- 1 cup sugar
- 1 can (5 ounces) evaporated milk
- 1/4 cup maple syrup
- 1/4 teaspoon vanilla extract

Preheat oven to 350 degrees. For cake, cream butter and sugar in a large bowl until fluffy. Add pumpkin, eggs, and vanilla; beat until well blended and smooth. In a medium bowl, combine flour, cinnamon, baking soda, cloves, and salt. Add dry ingredients, 1 cup at a time, to creamed mixture; beat until well blended. Stir in walnuts and raisins.

Spoon batter into a greased 10-inch fluted tube pan. Bake 55 to 65 minutes or until a toothpick inserted in center of cake comes out clean. Cool in pan 10 minutes. Invert onto a serving plate. Cool completely.

For icing, melt butter in a heavy medium saucepan over medium-high heat. Stir in sugar, evaporated milk, and maple syrup. Stirring constantly, bring mixture to a boil; boil 6 minutes. Remove from heat. Stir in vanilla. Pour into a medium bowl and cool 10 minutes. Beat 8 to 10 minutes or until thick and creamy. Spread icing over top of cake.

Yield: about 16 servings

OLD-TIME COUNTRY SUPPER

MENU

Peach Brandy Cordial	*Christmas Succotash*
Baked Onion Turnovers	*Green Bean and Mushroom Bake*
Creamy Peanut Soup	*Twice-Baked Sweet Potatoes*
Parsley Crackers	*Hot Cranberry-Lemon Tea*
Apple-Pecan Salad	*Fruited Rice Cream*
Festive Cabbage Slaw	*"Ragg Wool Mitten" Cookies*
Cornmeal-Molasses Bread	*Blackberry Jam Cake*
Fresh Ham with Cranberry Glaze	

Basted with a sweet, tangy sauce, Fresh Ham with Cranberry Glaze is succulent and tender. It's sure to become traditional holiday fare.

FRESH HAM WITH CRANBERRY GLAZE

You may need to special order your ham (also called a pork leg) from the butcher.

- 1 fresh whole ham (about 14 pounds), trimmed
- 1¹/₂ cups chopped onions
- ¹/₄ cup butter or margarine
- 2 cans (16 ounces each) whole berry cranberry sauce
- ²/₃ cup apple cider vinegar
- 4 teaspoons Worcestershire sauce
- ¹/₄ teaspoon hot pepper sauce
- ³/₄ cup firmly packed brown sugar
- 2 tablespoons dry mustard
- 1 tablespoon minced crystallized ginger

Preheat oven to 350 degrees. Place ham on a rack in a large roasting pan. Insert a meat thermometer into thickest portion of ham, making sure thermometer does not touch fat or bone. Cover and bake meat 18 to 20 minutes per pound or until thermometer registers 160 degrees.

For cranberry glaze, combine onions and butter in a medium saucepan; cook over medium heat about 10 minutes or until onions are tender. Stir in cranberry sauce, vinegar, Worcestershire sauce, and pepper sauce. Add brown sugar, dry mustard, and ginger; stir until well blended. Bring mixture to a boil. Reduce heat to medium-low; simmer 20 minutes or until mixture is slightly thickened. Uncover ham during last hour of baking; spoon glaze over ham every 15 minutes. Remove from oven and allow to stand 15 minutes before serving. Serve warm with remaining cranberry glaze.
Yield: 28 to 35 servings

A smooth before-dinner liqueur, Peach Brandy Cordial (recipe on page 78) offers rich, fruity flavor with a hint of anise. Baked Onion Turnovers are tasty little treats.

BAKED ONION TURNOVERS

PASTRY
- 2¹/₂ cups all-purpose flour
- 1 teaspoon dry mustard
- ¹/₂ teaspoon salt
- ¹/₈ teaspoon ground red pepper
- 2 packages (8 ounces each) cream cheese, softened
- ³/₄ cup butter or margarine, softened

FILLING
- 2 tablespoons butter or margarine
- 6 cups coarsely chopped yellow onions
- 2 tablespoons firmly packed brown sugar
- ¹/₂ teaspoon salt
- ¹/₄ teaspoon ground black pepper
- ¹/₄ teaspoon curry powder
- ¹/₈ teaspoon ground red pepper

For pastry, combine flour, dry mustard, salt, and red pepper in a medium bowl. Process cream cheese and butter in a food processor until blended. Add dry ingredients to creamed mixture and process just until blended. Divide dough into fourths and wrap in plastic wrap; chill 1 hour.

Preheat oven to 375 degrees. For filling, melt butter in a large skillet over medium-high heat. Add onions; cook just until onions soften. Stir in brown sugar. Continue to cook until onions are lightly browned and sugar is dissolved; remove from heat. Stir in salt, black pepper, curry powder, and red pepper. Roll out one fourth of dough into a 9-inch square. Cut into 3-inch squares. Place about 1 rounded teaspoon onion mixture in center of each square. Fold dough over filling to form a triangle; use a fork to crimp edges together. Turn pastries over and crimp edges again. Prick tops of pastries with a fork. Transfer to a lightly greased baking sheet. Bake 15 to 20 minutes or until lightly browned. Repeat with remaining dough and filling. Serve warm.
Yield: about 3 dozen appetizers

PEACH BRANDY CORDIAL

(Shown on page 77)

4 1/2   cups water
4   cups peach nectar
1   can (12 ounces) frozen orange
      juice concentrate, thawed
1   can (12 ounces) frozen white
      grape juice concentrate,
      thawed
1   cup peach brandy
1/2   teaspoon anise extract

In a 1-gallon container, combine water, peach nectar, juice concentrates, brandy, and anise extract. Cover and chill. Serve chilled.
Yield: about 12 1/2 cups cordial

PARSLEY CRACKERS

4   dozen saltine crackers
1/4   cup butter
3   tablespoons finely chopped fresh
      parsley

Preheat oven to 325 degrees. Place crackers on two 10 1/2 x 15 1/2-inch jellyroll pans. In a small saucepan, melt butter over medium heat. Remove from heat; stir in parsley. Brush butter mixture over crackers. Bake about 5 minutes or until lightly browned.
Yield: 4 dozen crackers

CREAMY PEANUT SOUP

1/4   cup butter or margarine
3/4   cup finely chopped onion
3/4   cup finely chopped celery
3   cloves garlic, minced
1/4   teaspoon crushed red pepper
      flakes
3   tablespoons all-purpose flour
6   cups chicken broth
1 1/2   cups smooth peanut butter
1   tablespoon soy sauce
      Coarsely chopped peanuts to
      garnish

In a large saucepan, melt butter over medium-high heat. Add onion, celery, garlic, and red pepper flakes. Cook 5 minutes or until vegetables are tender.

Peanut butter, soy sauce, and chicken broth give Creamy Peanut Soup its unusual and robust taste. Buttery Parsley Crackers are a terrific accompaniment — and simple to make, too!

Sprinkle flour over vegetable mixture. Stirring constantly, cook 1 minute or until well blended. Whisking constantly, add chicken broth, peanut butter, and soy sauce. Reduce heat to medium low; whisking frequently, simmer about 15 minutes. Garnish with peanuts and serve hot.
Yield: about 8 cups soup

APPLE-PECAN SALAD

6 cups unpeeled, coarsely
  chopped apples
2 tablespoons lemon juice
1/2 cup finely chopped celery
1/2 cup raisins
1/2 cup chopped pecans, toasted
1/2 cup sour cream
1/2 cup mayonnaise
6 tablespoons sugar
  Red leaf lettuce to serve

In a large bowl, toss apples and
lemon juice. Stir in celery, raisins, and
pecans. In a small bowl, combine sour
cream, mayonnaise, and sugar. Stir
sour cream mixture into apple mixture.
Cover and chill until ready to serve.
Serve in a lettuce-lined bowl.
Yield: about 7 cups salad

FESTIVE CABBAGE SLAW

11 cups finely shredded green
   cabbage
 8 cups finely shredded Savoy
   cabbage
 4 cups finely shredded Napa
   cabbage
2 1/4 cups finely chopped onions
 1 cup finely chopped green pepper
 1 cup finely chopped sweet red
   pepper
 3/4 cup finely shredded carrots
 2 cups sugar
1 1/4 cups apple cider vinegar
 1/3 cup vegetable oil
 1 tablespoon salt
 1 tablespoon celery seed
 1 teaspoon dry mustard
 1/2 teaspoon ground black pepper

In a very large bowl, combine
cabbages, onions, peppers, and
carrots. In a medium saucepan,
combine sugar, vinegar, oil, salt, celery
seed, dry mustard, and black pepper.
Stirring frequently, cook over medium-
high heat about 6 minutes or until
mixture comes to a boil. Pour hot
vinegar mixture over cabbage mixture.
Toss until vegetables are well coated.
Cover and chill 8 hours.
Yield: about 13 cups slaw

Cornmeal-Molasses Bread (clockwise from top left) *is a yeast bread with hearty texture. Festive Cabbage Slaw features a tangy celery seed vinaigrette. For a Waldorf salad with a twist, try Apple-Pecan Salad.*

CORNMEAL-MOLASSES BREAD

  Vegetable cooking spray
 1 cup plus 6 teaspoons yellow
   cornmeal, divided
2 1/2 cups water
 1/4 cup butter or margarine
 2 teaspoons salt
 1 package dry yeast
 1/2 cup warm water
 1/2 cup molasses
 1 egg
 5 to 6 cups all-purpose flour,
   divided

Spray two 1 1/2-quart ovenproof
bowls with cooking spray. Sprinkle
2 teaspoons cornmeal in each bowl,
turning to coat inside of each bowl
with cornmeal. In a medium
saucepan, bring 2 1/2 cups water to a
boil. Remove from heat; gradually
whisk in 1 cup cornmeal. Add butter
and salt; stir until butter melts. Let
cornmeal mixture cool 30 minutes.
In a small bowl, dissolve yeast in

1/2 cup warm water. In a large bowl,
combine cornmeal mixture, molasses,
egg, and yeast mixture. Add 5 cups
flour; stir until a soft dough forms.
Turn dough onto a lightly floured
surface. Knead about 5 minutes or
until dough becomes smooth and
elastic, using additional flour as
necessary. Divide dough in half and
place in prepared bowls. Spray tops
of dough with cooking spray. Sprinkle
remaining 2 teaspoons cornmeal on
tops of loaves. Let bread rise
uncovered in a warm place (80 to
85 degrees) 1 hour or until doubled
in size.

Preheat oven to 375 degrees. Bake
bread in bowls 43 to 50 minutes or
until bread is golden brown and
sounds hollow when tapped. Remove
from bowls; serve warm or transfer to
a wire rack to cool completely.
Yield: 2 round loaves

CHRISTMAS SUCCOTASH

15 slices bacon
³/₄ cup finely chopped onion
2 packages (10 ounces each) frozen whole kernel yellow corn, thawed
2 packages (10 ounces each) frozen baby lima beans, thawed
1 can (10 ounces) diced tomatoes and green chiles
1¹/₄ cups bread crumbs
2 cups half and half
3 eggs
1 tablespoon sugar
³/₄ teaspoon salt
¹/₄ teaspoon ground black pepper

Preheat oven to 375 degrees. In a heavy large skillet, cook bacon over medium heat until crisp. Transfer bacon to paper towels, reserving drippings in skillet. Set aside 6 slices bacon for garnish; crumble remaining bacon. Cook onion in bacon drippings until tender; drain onion. In a large bowl, combine crumbled bacon, onion, corn, lima beans, undrained tomatoes and green chiles, and bread crumbs. In a small bowl, beat half and half and eggs until blended; stir in sugar, salt, and pepper. Stir half and half mixture into vegetable mixture. Pour into a greased 9 x 13-inch baking dish. Cover and bake 1¹/₂ hours. Uncover and bake 15 minutes longer. Crumble remaining bacon over casserole to garnish; serve warm.
Yield: 12 to 14 servings

GREEN BEAN AND MUSHROOM BAKE

1 can (10³/₄ ounces) golden mushroom soup
2 cups (8 ounces) shredded Swiss cheese, divided
1 cup sour cream
2 tablespoons white wine
¹/₂ teaspoon salt
¹/₂ teaspoon lemon pepper
¹/₄ teaspoon ground black pepper
8 ounces fresh mushrooms, sliced

Spicy Twice-Baked Sweet Potatoes (clockwise from top left on plate) *feature pineapple and a cinnamony topping. Christmas Succotash adds a sprinkling of crumbled bacon to colorful vegetables. Green Bean and Mushroom Bake blends almonds, vegetables, and fresh mushrooms.*

³/₄ cup finely chopped onion
1 clove garlic, minced
3 tablespoons butter or margarine
3 cans (14¹/₂ ounces each) French-style green beans, drained
¹/₃ cup coarsely chopped slivered almonds

Preheat oven to 325 degrees. In a medium bowl, combine soup, 1 cup cheese, sour cream, wine, salt, lemon pepper, and black pepper. In a large skillet, sauté mushrooms, onion, and garlic in butter over medium heat just until vegetables are tender. Remove from heat and stir in green beans. Stir in soup mixture. Spoon mixture into a greased 9 x 13-inch baking dish. Sprinkle remaining 1 cup cheese over casserole. Sprinkle almonds over casserole. Bake 35 to 45 minutes or until casserole is heated through; serve warm.
Yield: 12 to 14 servings

TWICE-BAKED SWEET POTATOES

- 4 sweet potatoes
- 1/2 cup firmly packed brown sugar
- 1/4 cup butter or margarine, softened
- 1 can (8 ounces) crushed pineapple, drained
- 1/4 teaspoon ground cardamom
- 1/8 teaspoon ground ginger
- 1/8 teaspoon salt
- 1 cup bread crumbs
- 1/2 teaspoon ground cinnamon
- 2 tablespoons butter, melted

Preheat oven to 425 degrees. Trim ends and lightly grease potatoes. Bake 45 to 50 minutes or just until tender. Cool potatoes 30 minutes.

Preheat oven to 375 degrees. Cut potatoes in half lengthwise. Scoop out potato pulp, leaving about a 1/4-inch shell. In a medium bowl, combine potato pulp, brown sugar, butter, pineapple, cardamom, ginger, and salt; beat until well blended and fluffy. Spoon potato mixture into potato shells and place on an ungreased baking sheet. In a small bowl, combine bread crumbs and cinnamon. Add melted butter; stir until well blended. Spoon over potatoes. Bake stuffed potatoes 20 minutes or until heated through and topping is golden brown. Serve warm.

Yield: 8 servings

"RAGG WOOL MITTEN" COOKIES

COOKIES
- 2 cups all-purpose flour
- 1 cup chopped pecans, toasted
- 1/4 teaspoon salt
- 1 cup butter or margarine, softened
- 1/2 cup firmly packed brown sugar

ICING
- 1 1/2 cups confectioners sugar
- 3 tablespoons butter, softened
- 1 tablespoon plus 1 teaspoon milk

Our "Ragg Wool Mitten" Cookies have the old-fashioned flavor of pecan shortbread. The mitten-shaped cookies are decorated with piped-on icing.

- 1 teaspoon vanilla extract
  Ivory, brown, red, terra-cotta, kelly green, and juniper green paste food coloring

For cookies, process flour, pecans, and salt in a food processor until mixture becomes a fine powder. In a large bowl, cream butter and brown sugar until fluffy. Add dry ingredients to creamed mixture; stir until a soft dough forms. Divide dough in half and wrap in plastic wrap; chill 4 hours.

Preheat oven to 300 degrees. Trace pattern onto a piece of stencil plastic; cut out. On a lightly floured surface, use a floured rolling pin to roll out half of dough to 1/4-inch thickness. Use pattern and a sharp knife to cut out cookies. Transfer to a greased baking sheet. Bake 17 to 20 minutes or until bottoms are lightly browned. Cool cookies on baking sheet 3 minutes; transfer to a wire rack to cool completely. Repeat with remaining dough.

For icing, combine confectioners sugar, butter, milk, and vanilla in a small bowl; beat until smooth. Place 1/4 cup icing in a small bowl; tint beige using ivory and brown food coloring. Divide remaining icing between 2 small bowls; tint one bowl "country red" using red and terra-cotta food coloring and tint remaining icing "country green" using kelly and juniper green food coloring. Spoon icings into pastry bags fitted with small round tips. Pipe cuffs, hearts, and "blanket stitch" onto cookies. Use very small round tips to pipe lines and dots onto hearts. Pipe a circle of icing and fill in circle for each "button." Pipe icing onto top of each button for "thread." Allow icing to harden. Store in an airtight container in a single layer.

Yield: about 1 1/2 dozen cookies

HOT CRANBERRY-LEMON TEA

    8   cups boiling water
    4   regular-size tea bags
    1   stick cinnamon
1 1/4   cups sugar
    4   cups cranberry juice cocktail
  1/4   cup freshly squeezed lemon
        juice
        Cinnamon sticks to serve

In a heavy large Dutch oven, pour boiling water over tea bags and cinnamon stick; steep 5 minutes. Remove tea bags and cinnamon stick. Add sugar; stir until dissolved. Stir in cranberry juice cocktail and lemon juice. Place over medium heat until mixture is heated through. Serve hot with cinnamon sticks.
Yield: about 12 cups tea

FRUITED RICE CREAM

    1   jar (6 ounces) red maraschino
        cherries, drained
    1   jar (6 ounces) green
        maraschino cherries, drained
2 1/3   cups milk
    1   cup uncooked extra long-grain
        rice
  1/8   teaspoon salt
    2   cups miniature marshmallows
    1   package (8 ounces) cream
        cheese, cut into small pieces
        and softened
  1/2   cup sweetened condensed milk
  1/2   teaspoon almond extract
  1/2   teaspoon vanilla extract
    2   cups whipping cream, whipped
  1/2   cup sliced almonds

Chop cherries and drain on paper towels. Pat cherries dry and set aside. In a heavy medium saucepan, combine milk, rice, and salt over medium-low heat. Stirring frequently to prevent mixture from scorching, cover and cook about 25 to 30 minutes or until rice is tender and most of milk is absorbed. Remove from heat. Without stirring, add marshmallows and cream cheese to rice mixture; cover and let

Hot Cranberry-Lemon Tea is a fruity beverage that's perfect for warming guests on cold winter nights. Light, fluffy Fruited Rice Cream is a dreamy concoction with maraschino cherries and sliced almonds.

stand 5 minutes. Add sweetened condensed milk and extracts; stir until marshmallows melt and mixture is well blended. Transfer to a large bowl and cool 20 minutes.

Stir cherries into rice mixture. Fold in whipped cream and almonds. Spoon into individual serving dishes. Cover and chill until ready to serve.
Yield: about 8 cups fruited rice

A creamy custard crowns each moist layer of our Blackberry Jam Cake. This treat is so scrumptious, guests will insist on the recipe!

BLACKBERRY JAM CAKE

CAKE
- 1 cup butter or margarine, softened
- 2 cups sugar
- 4 eggs, separated
- 2 cups blackberry jam
- 3 cups all-purpose flour
- 1 teaspoon baking soda
- 1 teaspoon baking powder
- 1 teaspoon ground allspice
- 1 teaspoon ground cinnamon
- 1/8 teaspoon salt
- 1 cup buttermilk

CUSTARD
- 2 cups sugar
- 5 tablespoons all-purpose flour
- 1/8 teaspoon salt
- 1 1/2 cups milk
- 2 eggs
- 2 tablespoons butter or margarine

- 1 teaspoon vanilla extract
  Frozen whole blackberries to garnish

Preheat oven to 350 degrees. For cake, grease three 9-inch round cake pans and line bottoms with waxed paper; grease waxed paper. In a large bowl, cream butter and sugar until fluffy. Add egg yolks and jam; beat until smooth. In a medium bowl, combine flour, baking soda, baking powder, allspice, cinnamon, and salt. Alternately beat dry ingredients and buttermilk into creamed mixture, beating until well blended. In a small bowl, beat egg whites until stiff peaks form; fold into batter. Pour batter into prepared pans. Bake 28 to 33 minutes or until a toothpick inserted in center of cake comes out clean. Cool in pans

10 minutes. Remove from pans and cool completely on a wire rack.

For custard, combine sugar, flour, and salt in a heavy medium saucepan. Whisk in milk and eggs. Whisking constantly over medium heat, bring mixture to a boil; boil 2 minutes. Remove from heat. Whisk in butter and vanilla. Transfer mixture to a heatproof medium bowl. Set bowl in a larger bowl containing ice. Whisking occasionally, let mixture cool 10 minutes. Spread about 1 cup custard between each layer, spreading to edges. Spread remaining custard on top. Store in an airtight container in refrigerator. To serve, garnish with blackberries.

Yield: about 16 servings

GUILT-FREE CELEBRATION

If you're watching your waistline during the holidays, you'll want to browse through this collection of low-fat recipes. You'll find lots of light choices for a merry dinner party — from sparkling champagne punch to mouth-watering appetizers and main dishes. We've also included reduced-calorie desserts that you can enjoy guilt-free!

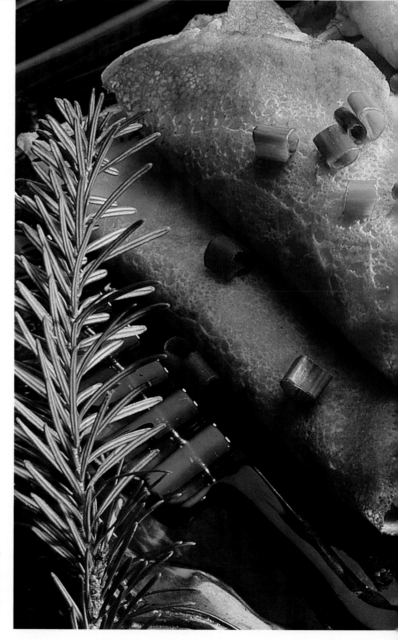

Delectable Salmon-Cream Cheese Crêpes (recipe on page 86) have a rich seafood filling. The elegant creations can be prepared ahead of time and baked just before serving.

SALMON-CREAM CHEESE CRÊPES (Shown on pages 84 and 85)

Crêpes can be assembled ahead of time and refrigerated.

CRÊPES

- ²/₃ cup all-purpose flour
- ¹/₄ teaspoon salt
- ¹/₄ teaspoon ground white pepper
- 1 cup evaporated skimmed milk
- 1 egg
- 1 tablespoon reduced-calorie margarine, melted
  Vegetable cooking spray

FILLING

- 1 package (8 ounces) fat-free cream cheese, softened
- 2 tablespoons finely chopped green onions
- 1¹/₂ tablespoons drained capers, rinsed
- 1 teaspoon dried basil leaves
- ¹/₄ teaspoon garlic powder
- ¹/₄ teaspoon ground white pepper
- 3 packages (3 ounces each) smoked salmon, broken into pieces
  Chopped green onion to garnish

For crêpes, combine flour, salt, and white pepper in a medium bowl. Add evaporated milk, egg, and melted margarine; whisk until smooth. Cover and chill 30 minutes.

Lightly spray an 8-inch nonstick skillet with cooking spray. Place pan over medium heat until hot. For each crêpe, spoon about 2 tablespoons batter into pan. Tilt pan to spread batter evenly over bottom of pan to form a 5-inch circle. Cook until lightly browned; turn over and cook

30 seconds longer. Place crêpes between layers of waxed paper.

For filling, combine cream cheese, 2 tablespoons chopped green onions, capers, basil, garlic powder, and white pepper in a medium bowl. Gently stir in salmon. Fill each crêpe with about 2 tablespoons salmon mixture. Roll up crêpes and place, seam side down, in a 9 x 13-inch baking dish. Cover and store crêpes in refrigerator until ready to serve.

To serve, bake covered 20 minutes in a 350-degree oven. Garnish with green onion and serve warm.
Yield: about 12 crêpes

1 serving (1 crêpe): 97 calories, 2.1 grams fat, 9.7 grams protein, 9.2 grams carbohydrate

Quick and easy to prepare, zesty Shrimp Salsa is bursting with flavor. Served with fat-free tortilla chips, the zippy appetizer is a delightful low-calorie treat.

SHRIMP SALSA

2½ pounds shrimp, cooked, peeled, deveined, and chopped (about 5 cups)
1 jar (24 ounces) mild chunky-style salsa
2 cups chopped fresh cilantro
2 cups finely chopped fresh tomatoes
¼ cup finely chopped red onion
2 tablespoons lime juice
Purchased fat-free tortilla chips to serve

In a large bowl, combine shrimp, salsa, cilantro, tomatoes, onion, and lime juice. Cover and refrigerate 8 hours or overnight to allow flavors to blend. Serve with tortilla chips.
Yield: about 8 cups salsa or 32 servings

1 serving (¼ cup salsa): 53 calories, 1.1 grams fat, 8.6 grams protein, 2.6 grams carbohydrate

SALMON PATÉ

1 container (16 ounces) plain fat-free yogurt
1 can (7½ ounces) skinless red salmon, drained and bones removed
1 cup (4 ounces) shredded fat-free Cheddar cheese
¼ cup fat-free honey Dijon mustard salad dressing
2 teaspoons prepared horseradish
½ teaspoon dried dill weed
½ teaspoon garlic powder
½ teaspoon salt
¼ teaspoon ground black pepper
¼ teaspoon onion powder
Fresh dill weed to garnish
Crackers or cucumber slices to serve

Line a wire strainer with cheesecloth or a coffee filter and place strainer over a medium bowl. Spoon yogurt into strainer. Cover with plastic wrap and refrigerate 24 hours to drain. Discard liquid.
In a medium bowl, combine yogurt

A delicious addition to a holiday buffet, Basil-Dill Cheese Ball is a savory combination of herbs and cheeses. Piquant Salmon Pâté features horseradish, garlic, and dill weed.

solids, salmon, cheese, salad dressing, horseradish, dill weed, garlic powder, salt, pepper, and onion powder; stir until well blended. Cover and refrigerate until well chilled. Shape into about a 9-inch-long roll. Garnish with fresh dill weed. Serve with crackers or cucumber slices.
Yield: about 2 cups paté or 8 servings

1 serving (¼ cup paté): 102 calories, 1.7 grams fat, 12.5 grams protein, 7.5 grams carbohydrate

BASIL-DILL CHEESE BALL

2 cups (8 ounces) finely shredded farmer cheese
1 cup fat-free cottage cheese
½ cup finely chopped green onions
¼ cup grated Parmesan cheese
1 tablespoon dried basil leaves, crushed
2 teaspoons dried dill weed
Chopped fresh cilantro leaves
Crackers to serve

In a medium bowl, combine farmer cheese, cottage cheese, green onions, Parmesan cheese, basil, and dill weed. Shape into a ball. Wrap in plastic wrap and refrigerate 8 hours or overnight to allow flavors to blend.
To serve, roll cheese ball in cilantro leaves. Let stand at room temperature 20 to 30 minutes or until cheese softens. Serve with crackers.
Yield: 1 cheese ball or 32 servings

1 serving (1 tablespoon cheese ball): 29 calories, 1.2 grams fat, 3.2 grams protein, 0.7 gram carbohydrate

BREADED VEGETABLES WITH MARINARA SAUCE

SAUCE

Olive oil cooking spray
1 cup finely chopped sweet red pepper
1/2 cup finely chopped onion
1 clove garlic, minced
1 can (29 ounces) tomato sauce
1 can (14 1/2 ounces) Italian-style stewed tomatoes, undrained
1 teaspoon dried parsley flakes
1 teaspoon sugar
1/2 teaspoon dried oregano leaves
1/2 teaspoon dried basil leaves
1/2 teaspoon dried thyme leaves
1/2 teaspoon salt
1/4 teaspoon ground black pepper
Shredded Parmesan cheese to garnish

BREADED VEGETABLES

1 1/2 cups finely crushed corn flake cereal
1/2 cup grated Parmesan cheese
1 teaspoon paprika
1/2 teaspoon salt
4 egg whites, beaten
4 large carrots, cut into 1/2 x 3-inch sticks
2 medium zucchini, cut into 1/2 x 3-inch sticks
8 ounces whole fresh mushrooms
Olive oil cooking spray

For sauce, spray a large saucepan with cooking spray. Combine red pepper, onion, and garlic in saucepan. Cook over medium heat until onion is tender. Add remaining ingredients; stir until well blended. Bring to a boil. Reduce heat to low; cover and simmer 30 minutes. Keep warm until ready to serve.

For breaded vegetables, preheat oven to 375 degrees. In a medium bowl, combine cereal, cheese, paprika, and salt. Place egg whites in a shallow bowl. Dip vegetables, one at a time, in egg whites. Coat with cereal mixture. Place on a baking sheet sprayed with cooking spray. Bake 20 to 25 minutes or until golden brown. Transfer sauce to a serving bowl and garnish with shredded cheese. Serve vegetables with sauce.

Yield: about 8 dozen pieces of vegetable and 5 1/2 cups sauce or 20 servings

1 serving (5 pieces of vegetable and 1/4 cup sauce): 61 calories, 1.0 gram fat, 3.6 grams protein, 10.7 grams carbohydrate

HORSERADISH BEEF ROLLS

1/2 cup fat-free cottage cheese
2 tablespoons prepared horseradish
2 teaspoons Dijon-style mustard
1 pound thinly sliced lean cooked roast beef
2 cans (10 biscuits each) refrigerated buttermilk biscuits
Vegetable cooking spray

Preheat oven to 450 degrees. For sauce, process cottage cheese, horseradish, and mustard in a small food processor until smooth. Cut or fold each slice of roast beef into a 3-inch square. On a lightly floured surface, use a floured rolling pin to roll each biscuit into a 4-inch square. Spread a heaping teaspoonful of sauce over biscuit. Place two 3-inch squares

Breaded Vegetables to serve with Marinara Sauce are baked instead of fried for a healthier snack. Horseradish Beef Rolls are easy to make by placing thin slices of roast beef and a creamy spread inside a fluffy biscuit wrapper.

of roast beef over sauce. Roll up biscuit and place, seam side down, on a baking sheet sprayed with cooking spray. Bake 8 to 10 minutes or until golden brown. Serve warm with remaining sauce.

Yield: 20 beef rolls

1 serving (1 beef roll): 105 calories, 3.2 grams fat, 8.9 grams protein, 10.5 grams carbohydrate

CHAMPAGNE PUNCH

1 bottle (64 ounces) cranberry juice cocktail, chilled
1 can (12 ounces) frozen pineapple juice concentrate, thawed
2 cups brandy
2 bottles (750 ml each) champagne, chilled

Combine cranberry juice, pineapple juice, and brandy in a large punch bowl. Stir in champagne. Serve immediately.

Yield: about 18 cups punch

1 serving (6 ounces): 164 calories, 0.1 gram fat, 0.3 gram protein, 19.7 grams carbohydrate

ARTICHOKE-PARMESAN PUFFS

1 cup water
2 tablespoons reduced-calorie margarine
1 cup all-purpose flour
1 teaspoon garlic salt
1/2 cup egg substitute
1 egg
1 can (14 ounces) artichoke hearts, drained and finely chopped
1/4 cup grated fat-free Parmesan cheese

Preheat oven to 375 degrees. Bring water and margarine to a boil in a large saucepan. Reduce heat to low. Add flour and garlic salt all at once, stirring vigorously until mixture forms a ball; remove from heat. Add egg substitute and egg; beat until well

For a refreshing zing, Champagne Punch combines fruit juices, brandy, and chilled bubbly. Cheesy Artichoke-Parmesan Puffs are great grab-as-you-go appetizers, and Light Cucumber-Dill Dip will be a crowd-pleaser.

blended. Beat in artichoke hearts and cheese. Drop heaping teaspoonfuls of batter onto a baking sheet lined with parchment paper. Bake 25 to 28 minutes or until lightly browned. Serve warm.

Yield: about 5 dozen appetizers

1 serving (1 appetizer): 17 calories, 0.4 gram fat, 0.7 gram protein, 2.6 grams carbohydrate

LIGHT CUCUMBER-DILL DIP

4 ounces fat-free cream cheese
1/2 cup fat-free cottage cheese
1 tablespoon chopped green onion
2 teaspoons freshly squeezed lemon juice
3/4 teaspoon salt
1/2 teaspoon chopped fresh dill weed
1/8 teaspoon ground black pepper
1 cucumber peeled, seeded, and coarsely chopped
Fresh vegetables to serve

Process cream cheese, cottage cheese, green onion, lemon juice, salt, dill weed, and black pepper in a food processor until smooth. Add cucumber; pulse process just until blended. Cover and chill 2 hours to allow flavors to blend. Serve with fresh vegetables.

Yield: about 2 cups dip

1 serving (1 tablespoon dip): 7 calories, 0 gram fat, 1.1 grams protein, 0.7 gram carbohydrate

SHRIMP BUNDLES

- 1 package (8 ounces) fat-free cream cheese, softened
- ¼ cup cooking sherry
- ¼ cup finely chopped green onions
- 1 teaspoon dried tarragon leaves, crushed
- ½ teaspoon garlic powder
- ½ teaspoon salt
- ½ teaspoon ground black pepper
- 9 sheets frozen phyllo pastry, thawed according to package directions
  Olive oil cooking spray
- 3 dozen medium shrimp, cooked, peeled, and deveined

Preheat oven to 375 degrees. In a medium bowl, combine cream cheese, sherry, onions, tarragon, garlic powder, salt, and pepper; stir until well blended.

Lightly spray each sheet of phyllo pastry with cooking spray. Stack 3 sheets of pastry on top of each other; cut into twelve 4-inch squares. Spoon a heaping teaspoonful of cheese mixture in center of each pastry square. Place 1 shrimp over cheese mixture on each pastry square. Bring corners of pastry squares together and twist. Place on a baking sheet sprayed with cooking spray. Lightly spray each bundle with cooking spray. Repeat with remaining pastry sheets, cheese mixture, and shrimp. Bake 6 to 8 minutes or until lightly browned. Serve warm.

Yield: 3 dozen shrimp bundles

1 serving (1 shrimp bundle): 38 calories, 0.2 gram fat, 4.3 grams protein, 4.0 grams carbohydrate

CUCUMBER DIP

- 1 large cucumber, peeled and seeded
- 1 container (8 ounces) fat-free cottage cheese
- ¼ cup chopped pecans
- 1 teaspoon lemon juice
- 1 package (1 ounce) fat-free ranch salad dressing mix
- 2 tablespoons fat-free mayonnaise
- 1 teaspoon garlic powder
- 1 teaspoon onion powder
  Small carrot and fresh parsley to garnish
  Fresh vegetables to serve

Process cucumber, cottage cheese, pecans, lemon juice, dressing mix, mayonnaise, garlic powder, and onion powder in a food processor until cucumber and pecans are finely

Flaky pastry wrappers encase shrimp and a creamy filling to create these wonderful Shrimp Bundles. Light, cool Cucumber Dip makes a colorful appetizer when paired with fresh vegetables.

chopped. Transfer to an airtight container and refrigerate until well chilled. Garnish with carrot and parsley. Serve with fresh vegetables.

Yield: about 2 cups dip or 16 servings

1 serving (2 tablespoons dip): 33 calories, 1.2 grams fat, 1.9 grams protein, 4.0 grams carbohydrate

CRANBERRY-PEAR AMBROSIA

1¼ cups 2% milk, divided
  2 tablespoons cornstarch
¼ cup sugar
½ cup frozen unsweetened shredded coconut, thawed
  3 cups unpeeled, cored, and coarsely chopped red pears
⅔ cup sweetened dried cranberries
  1 tablespoon frozen unsweetened flaked coconut, thawed and toasted to garnish

In a small bowl, combine ¼ cup milk and cornstarch; stir until smooth. In a medium saucepan, combine sugar and remaining 1 cup milk; bring to a simmer over medium heat. Whisking constantly, add cornstarch mixture; cook until sauce thickens. Remove from heat; cool.

Stir in ½ cup coconut. Gently combine coconut sauce, pears, and cranberries. Cover and refrigerate until well chilled. Garnish with toasted coconut.

Yield: about 8 servings

1 serving (½ cup): 135 calories, 3.9 grams fat, 1.8 grams protein, 24.5 grams carbohydrate

HAM HASH

    Vegetable cooking spray
  1 cup chopped onion
  4 cups diced unpeeled red potatoes
  2 cups thinly sliced and chopped low-fat ham
  1 can (4½ ounces) chopped green chiles
¼ cup low-fat sour cream
¾ teaspoon garlic salt
½ teaspoon ground cumin

Cranberry-Pear Ambrosia (clockwise from bottom) *is served in a dreamy coconut sauce. Spicy Ham Hash is complemented by zesty Brussels Sprouts in Light Orange Sauce* (recipe on page 95). *Replace traditional stuffing with zesty Caesar Bread Salad (not shown), a colorful concoction of fresh tomatoes, cucumber, and herbed stuffing.*

Spray a large nonstick skillet with cooking spray. Sauté onion in skillet over medium-high heat until onion is tender and begins to brown. Reduce heat to medium. Stir in potatoes. Stirring occasionally, cook about 25 minutes or until potatoes are golden brown and almost tender. Stir in ham, undrained chiles, sour cream, garlic salt, and cumin. Stirring occasionally, cook about 5 minutes or until mixture is heated through. Serve warm.

Yield: about 11 servings

1 serving (½ cup): 91 calories, 2.0 grams fat, 6.4 grams protein, 11.9 grams carbohydrate

CAESAR BREAD SALAD

  1 package (8 ounces) herb-seasoned stuffing

  5 cups chopped fresh tomatoes
1½ cups shredded unpeeled cucumber
  1 cup chopped fresh parsley
  1 cup fat-free Caesar salad dressing
  1 tablespoon balsamic vinegar
  1 tablespoon olive oil

Combine stuffing, tomatoes, cucumber, and parsley; stir gently. In a small bowl, combine salad dressing, vinegar, and oil. Stir dressing mixture into salad. Cover and chill 2 hours; serve within 4 hours.

Yield: about 18 servings

1 serving (½ cup): 82 calories, 1.4 grams fat, 2.0 grams protein, 15.3 grams carbohydrate

SCALLOPS AND PROSCIUTTO

- 10 ounces thinly sliced prosciutto
- 2 pounds sea scallops
- 1 cup freshly squeezed lemon juice
- 1/4 cup honey
- 1/4 cup soy sauce
- 4 cloves garlic, minced
- 2 teaspoons dried tarragon leaves, crushed
- 1 teaspoon salt
- 1/2 teaspoon ground black pepper
  Olive oil cooking spray
- 2 teaspoons cornstarch
- 2 teaspoons water

Cut prosciutto into 1/2 x 4-inch strips. Wrap each scallop with 1 strip of prosciutto and secure with a toothpick. In a medium bowl, combine lemon juice, honey, soy sauce, garlic, tarragon, salt, and pepper. Add scallops, cover, and refrigerate 8 hours or overnight to allow flavors to blend.

Spray a large skillet with cooking spray. Heat skillet over medium heat. Reserving lemon juice mixture, use a slotted spoon to place scallops in heated skillet and cook 5 to 8 minutes or until lightly browned, turning once. Place scallops on a serving dish, cover, and keep warm until ready to serve.

In a small bowl, combine cornstarch and water; stir until smooth. Pour reserved lemon juice mixture into a small saucepan. Bring to a boil. Stirring constantly, add cornstarch mixture and cook 5 to 8 minutes or until thickened. Serve with scallops.

Yield: about 5 dozen appetizers

1 serving (1 ounce or 2 to 3 scallops): 71 calories, 1.4 grams fat, 9.4 grams protein, 5.0 grams carbohydrate

STUFFED POTATOES

- 10 small russet potatoes, baked
- 2 cups fat-free cottage cheese
- 1 teaspoon salt
- 1/4 teaspoon ground black pepper
- 2 tablespoons reduced-calorie margarine
- 1 cup finely chopped onions

For a taste-tempting treat, tender scallops are wrapped in thin slices of prosciutto and dipped in a warm, tangy sauce. Scrumptious Stuffed Potatoes feature a flavorful mushroom and onion filling topped with cheese and chives.

1 cup chopped fresh mushrooms
1 clove garlic, minced
Vegetable cooking spray
2 cups (8 ounces) finely shredded
fat-free Cheddar cheese
1/4 cup chopped fresh chives

Preheat oven to 375 degrees. Cut potatoes in half lengthwise. Leaving about 1/2 inch of pulp on skins, scoop out remaining pulp and place in a large bowl. Add cottage cheese, salt, and pepper to potato pulp; stir until well blended and set aside.

In a medium skillet, melt margarine over medium heat. Add onions, mushrooms, and garlic; cook until onions are tender. Add onion mixture to potato mixture; stir until well blended. Spoon mixture into potato skins and place on a baking sheet sprayed with cooking spray. Sprinkle cheese and chives evenly over stuffed potatoes. Bake 8 to 10 minutes or until cheese is bubbly. Serve warm.

Yield: 20 stuffed potato halves

1 serving (1/2 potato): 96 calories, 0.7 gram fat, 7.1 grams protein, 15.2 grams carbohydrate

OVEN-FRIED CHICKEN

2 pounds boneless skinless
chicken breast fillets
Salt and ground black pepper
1 1/2 cups plain nonfat yogurt
1/2 cup grated Parmesan cheese
1 teaspoon paprika
1 teaspoon dried thyme leaves
1/2 teaspoon garlic powder
1 1/2 cups plain bread crumbs
3 tablespoons butter or margarine,
melted

Preheat oven to 400 degrees. Sprinkle chicken with salt and pepper. In a small bowl, whisk yogurt, cheese, paprika, thyme, and garlic powder. In another small bowl, combine bread crumbs and butter. Dip chicken, one piece at a time, into yogurt mixture, then place in bread crumb mixture. Spoon bread crumb mixture over chicken, coating well. Place coated

Tasty Barley-Vegetable Salad is a blend of crunchy vegetables, calcium-rich feta cheese, and nourishing barley. Delicious cold, Oven-Fried Chicken (not shown) features a zesty herbed breading.

pieces of chicken in a greased baking pan. Bake 25 to 30 minutes or until juices run clear when thickest part of chicken is pierced with a fork. Cover and refrigerate until ready to serve. Serve cold.

Yield: about 6 servings

1 serving (1 chicken fillet): 389 calories, 11.6 grams fat, 44.4 grams protein, 25.2 grams carbohydrate

BARLEY-VEGETABLE SALAD

4 cups water
1 cup uncooked barley
3/4 cup finely diced radishes
3/4 cup finely diced carrots
1/2 cup peeled and finely diced
cucumber
1/4 cup finely chopped fresh parsley
2 tablespoons finely chopped red
onion
2 tablespoons finely chopped fresh
chives
1/2 cup oil-free Italian salad dressing

2 tablespoons lemon juice
2 teaspoons dried oregano leaves,
crushed
1/2 teaspoon garlic powder
1/4 teaspoon salt
1/4 teaspoon ground black pepper
7 ounces feta cheese, crumbled

In a 3-quart saucepan, bring water to a boil; stir in barley. Reduce heat to low; cover and simmer 50 to 55 minutes or until tender. Remove from heat; cool to room temperature.

In a large bowl, combine cooked barley, radishes, carrots, cucumber, parsley, onion, and chives. In a small bowl, whisk salad dressing, lemon juice, oregano, garlic powder, salt, and pepper. Pour over barley mixture; stir until well blended. Stir in cheese. Cover and refrigerate until ready to serve.

Yield: about 7 1/2 cups salad

1 serving (1/2 cup): 88 calories, 3.6 grams fat, 3.8 grams protein, 10.7 grams carbohydrate

CREAMY CELERY SOUP

6 cups coarsely chopped celery
5 cups peeled and coarsely
    chopped potatoes
1 cup chopped green onions
3 cans (14½ ounces each)
    fat-free chicken broth
2 tablespoons freshly squeezed
    lemon juice
1 teaspoon dried tarragon leaves
¾ teaspoon salt
½ teaspoon ground white pepper
1 cup plain low-fat yogurt
2 teaspoons cornstarch
    Celery leaves to garnish

In a large Dutch oven, combine celery, potatoes, onions, and chicken broth. Cover and cook over medium-low heat 1 hour or until vegetables are tender. Reserving broth, use a slotted spoon to transfer vegetables to a food processor; purée vegetables. Return puréed vegetables to broth in Dutch oven. Stir in lemon juice, tarragon leaves, salt, and white pepper. Cover and cook over medium-low heat 10 minutes or until mixture begins to simmer (do not boil). Remove soup from heat. In a small bowl, whisk yogurt and cornstarch until well blended. Gradually stir yogurt mixture into soup. Garnish with celery leaves. Serve immediately.
Yield: about 12 cups soup

1 serving (¾ cup): 69 calories, 0.7 gram fat, 2.9 grams protein, 13.6 grams carbohydrate

PARMESAN BREAD STICKS

1 package dry yeast
1 teaspoon sugar
1¼ cups warm water
2½ to 2¾ cups all-purpose flour,
    divided
½ teaspoon salt
1 tablespoon olive oil
    Vegetable cooking spray
2 tablespoons freshly grated
    Parmesan cheese

In a small bowl, dissolve yeast and sugar in warm water. In a large bowl, combine 1 cup flour and salt. Add yeast mixture and oil to dry ingredients; beat with an electric mixer about 3 minutes. Add 1½ cups flour; stir until well blended. Turn dough onto a lightly floured surface. Knead about 5 minutes or until dough becomes smooth and elastic, using remaining flour as necessary. Place in a large bowl sprayed with cooking spray, turning once to coat top of dough. Cover and let rise in a warm place (80 to 85 degrees) 1 hour or until doubled in size.

Turn dough onto a lightly floured surface and punch down. Roll dough into a 12 x 16-inch rectangle. Cut dough into 1 x 12-inch strips. Twist and press ends onto an ungreased baking sheet. Lightly brush strips with water. Sprinkle with Parmesan cheese. Lightly cover strips and let rise in a warm place 45 minutes or until almost doubled in size.

Preheat oven to 400 degrees. Bake 12 to 17 minutes or until bottoms are lightly browned. Serve warm.
Yield: 16 bread sticks

1 serving (1 bread stick): 92 calories, 1.3 grams fat, 2.7 grams protein, 16.9 grams carbohydrate

You'll love these two terrific meal starters: Creamy Celery Soup, seasoned with tarragon, and homemade Parmesan Bread Sticks!

BACON-CHEESE RISOTTO

> 2 cans (14¹/₂ ounces each)
>   fat-free chicken broth
> 3 cups water
>   Vegetable cooking spray
> 1 package (8 ounces) fresh
>   mushrooms, sliced
> 1¹/₄ cups chopped sweet red pepper
> 2 teaspoons minced garlic
> 2 cups uncooked Arborio rice
> ¹/₂ teaspoon salt
> 1 cup (4 ounces) shredded
>   reduced-fat sharp Cheddar
>   cheese
> 6 slices turkey bacon, cooked and
>   crumbled

Combine broth and water in a medium saucepan; bring to a simmer (do not boil). Keep warm. In a large saucepan sprayed with cooking spray, sauté mushrooms, red pepper, and garlic over medium-high heat about 5 minutes or until tender. Stirring constantly, add rice and cook 2 minutes. Reduce heat to medium low. Add salt and 1 cup broth mixture; stir constantly until most of liquid is absorbed. Add remaining broth mixture, ¹/₂ cup at a time, stirring after each addition until liquid is absorbed and rice has a creamy consistency (about 35 minutes). Stir in cheese and bacon; serve immediately.

Yield: about 15 servings

1 serving (¹/₂ cup): 119 calories, 1.8 grams fat, 5.7 grams protein, 20.1 grams carbohydrate

BRUSSELS SPROUTS WITH LIGHT ORANGE SAUCE

> 3 pounds fresh Brussels sprouts
> ³/₄ cup freshly squeezed orange juice
> 6 tablespoons fat-free Italian salad
>   dressing
> 1¹/₂ teaspoons grated orange zest
>   Grated orange zest to garnish

Trim Brussels sprouts and cut an "X" in stem end of each sprout. Place in a steamer basket over simmering water.

Brussels Sprouts with Light Orange Sauce (from left) are splashed with citrus flavor, and Bacon-Cheese Risotto is a low-fat version of an Italian favorite. Congealed Beets and Carrots are an eye-catching addition.

CONGEALED BEETS AND CARROTS

> 1 jar (16 ounces) pickled beets
> 1 package (3 ounces) lemon
>   gelatin
> 1 cup hot water
> 1 tablespoon apple cider vinegar
> ¹/₄ teaspoon salt
> ²/₃ cup diced celery
> ²/₃ cup finely shredded carrots
> 1 tablespoon grated onion
> 2 teaspoons prepared horseradish
> ¹/₈ teaspoon ground black pepper
>   Carrot curl to garnish

Reserving liquid, drain beets and chop. Add water to reserved beet liquid to make 1 cup. Place gelatin in a medium bowl. Add hot water; stir until dissolved. Add beet liquid, vinegar, and salt. Chill about 45 minutes or until slightly thickened.

Fold in beets, celery, carrots, onion, horseradish, and pepper. Pour into an oiled 1-quart mold. Cover and chill until firm.

To serve, dip mold into warm water 10 seconds; invert onto a serving plate. Garnish with carrot curl.

Yield: about 8 servings

1 serving (¹/₂ cup): 84 calories, 0.1 gram fat, 1.5 grams protein, 20.5 grams carbohydrate

Continued on page 96

Cover and steam about 15 minutes or until sprouts are tender. In a small bowl, combine orange juice, salad dressing, and 1 1/2 teaspoons orange zest. Toss sprouts with orange sauce. Transfer to a serving dish. Garnish with orange zest. Serve warm.
Yield: about 16 servings

1 serving (1/2 cup): 45 calories, 0.3 gram fat, 3.0 grams protein, 9.4 grams carbohydrate

CHICKEN PUFFS

PUFFS
- 1 cup all-purpose flour
- 1 teaspoon garlic powder
- 1/2 teaspoon salt
- 1/8 teaspoon ground red pepper
- 1 cup water
- 2 tablespoons reduced-calorie margarine
- 3 eggs
  Vegetable cooking spray

FILLING
- 2 tablespoons reduced-calorie margarine
- 1 cup evaporated skimmed milk, divided
- 2 tablespoons all-purpose flour
- 1/2 teaspoon salt
- 1/2 teaspoon ground black pepper
- 2 cans (5 ounces each) chicken, drained
- 1/2 cup peeled and diced cucumber
- 1/4 cup chopped green onions
- 2 tablespoons white cooking wine

For puffs, preheat oven to 400 degrees. In a small bowl, combine flour, garlic powder, salt, and pepper; set aside. In a medium saucepan, combine water and margarine. Bring to a boil. Reduce heat to low and gradually stir in flour mixture. Stirring constantly, cook until mixture begins to pull away from sides of pan. Remove from heat; cool 5 minutes. Using high speed of an electric mixer, add eggs, one at a time, beating well after each addition. Drop heaping tablespoonfuls of batter onto a baking sheet sprayed with cooking spray, mounding each

Chunks of ham, green onion, and jalapeño pepper add hearty flavor to Hot Spinach Dip. Chicken Puffs filled with a delectable mixture of chicken, cucumber, and green onion are tasty little morsels.

spoonful slightly in center. Bake 18 to 20 minutes or until golden brown and puffy. Transfer to a wire rack to cool completely.

For filling, melt margarine in a medium saucepan over medium heat. Stirring constantly, add 2 tablespoons milk, flour, salt, and pepper; cook 2 minutes. Stirring constantly, gradually add remaining milk; cook until thickened. Stir in chicken, cucumber, onions, and wine. Cook about 2 minutes or until heated through. Using a sharp knife, carefully slice tops off puffs. Spoon about 1 tablespoon filling onto bottom halves of puffs; replace tops. Serve warm.
Yield: about 2 dozen puffs

1 serving (1 puff): 68 calories, 2.1 grams fat, 5.9 grams protein, 5.8 grams carbohydrate

HOT SPINACH DIP

- 1 package (10 ounces) frozen chopped spinach, thawed and well drained
- 1/2 pound cooked lean ham, diced
- 1 cup (4 ounces) shredded fat-free mozzarella cheese
- 1/2 cup fat-free sour cream
- 3 ounces fat-free cream cheese, softened
- 1/4 cup chopped green onions
- 1 tablespoon prepared horseradish
- 1 fresh jalapeño pepper, seeded and minced
- 1 teaspoon salt
- 1/2 teaspoon ground black pepper
  Vegetable cooking spray
  Fat-free sour cream and green onion to garnish
  Pita bread, cut in wedges, to serve

Preheat oven to 375 degrees. In a large bowl, combine spinach, ham, mozzarella cheese, sour cream, cream cheese, green onions, horseradish, jalapeño pepper, salt, and black pepper. Spread mixture into a 9-inch pie plate sprayed with cooking spray. Bake 15 to 18 minutes or until heated through. Garnish with sour cream and green onion. Serve warm with pita bread.

Yield: about 3 cups dip or 9 servings

1 serving (¹/₃ cup dip): 85 calories, 1.5 grams fat, 13.6 grams protein, 3.2 grams carbohydrate

ORANGE TART

CRUST

- 1   tablespoon light corn syrup
- 1   tablespoon water
- 1¹/₂ cups graham cracker crumbs
- 2   teaspoons butter or margarine, chilled
- ¹/₂ teaspoon ground cinnamon
     Vegetable cooking spray

FILLING

- 1   envelope unflavored gelatin
- ¹/₂ cup orange juice
- 1   package (8 ounces) Neufchâtel cheese
- 1   container (8 ounces) nonfat vanilla yogurt
- 1   teaspoon grated orange zest
- 1   packet (.035 ounce) sugar substitute (equivalent to 2 teaspoons sugar)
- ¹/₂ teaspoon clear vanilla extract
- 3   cans (11 ounces each) mandarin oranges, well drained
- 3   tablespoons orange marmalade

Preheat oven to 375 degrees. For crust, combine corn syrup and water in a small bowl until well blended. In a food processor, combine cracker crumbs, butter, and cinnamon. Add corn syrup mixture to processor. Process until ingredients are well blended. Press cracker crumb mixture into bottom and up sides of an 8 by 11-inch tart pan lightly sprayed with cooking spray. Bake 7 to 9 minutes

No one will believe that this refreshing Orange Tart is a low-calorie, low-fat dessert — but it is! Flavorful mandarin oranges cover the creamy filling that's prepared with Neufchâtel cheese, nonfat yogurt, and sugar substitute.

or until lightly browned and firm. Place pan on a wire rack to cool completely.

For filling, sprinkle gelatin over orange juice in a small saucepan; let stand 1 minute. Stirring constantly, cook over low heat about 5 minutes or until gelatin dissolves; remove from heat and allow to cool. Process Neufchâtel cheese, yogurt, orange zest, sugar substitute, vanilla, and gelatin mixture in a food processor until well blended and smooth. Pour

cheese mixture into crust. Cover and chill 1 hour or until filling is set.

To serve, remove sides of tart pan. Place orange segments on filling. Melt marmalade in a small saucepan over medium heat; brush segments with melted marmalade. Serve immediately.

Yield: about 12 servings

1 serving (¹/₁₂ of tart): 196 calories, 6.6 grams fat, 5.0 grams protein, 29.7 grams carbohydrate

Light and crispy, Cinnamon Popcorn Snack Mix is sure to be a crowd-pleaser. Featuring layers of angel food cake and reduced-fat ice cream, Praline Ice Cream Cake is proof that a low-calorie dessert can be delicious, too! Maraschino cherries frozen in ice cubes add a festive look to our fruity Christmas Tea.

CINNAMON POPCORN SNACK MIX

10   cups popped popcorn without salt or fat
2   egg whites
1   cup sugar
1   teaspoon ground cinnamon
1   teaspoon salt

Preheat oven to 225 degrees. Place popcorn in a large bowl. In a small bowl, beat egg whites until stiff. Beat in sugar, cinnamon, and salt. Spoon egg white mixture over popcorn; stir until well coated. Spread evenly on a greased baking sheet. Bake 1 hour, stirring every 15 minutes. Cool completely on pan. Store in an airtight container.

Yield: about 8 cups snack mix

1 serving (1 cup snack mix):
126 calories, 0 gram fat, 2.1 grams protein, 30.3 grams carbohydrate

PRALINE ICE CREAM CAKE

1   angel food cake
4   cups reduced-fat praline and caramel ice cream, softened
1   container (12½ ounces) caramel ice cream topping, divided

Cut cake horizontally into thirds. Spread about 2 cups ice cream between each layer of cake. Drizzle about ¼ cup topping over top of cake. Cover and freeze until firm. To serve, cut into slices and drizzle with remaining topping.

Yield: about 16 servings

1 serving (¹⁄₁₆ of recipe):
217 calories, 1.4 grams fat, 5.9 grams protein, 46.2 grams carbohydrate

CHRISTMAS TEA

Maraschino cherries with stems, drained and frozen in ice cubes
2   quarts water, divided
3   large tea bags
1   can (6 ounces) frozen orange juice concentrate, thawed
2   teaspoons orange extract
12   packets sugar substitute

In a large saucepan or Dutch oven, bring 1 quart water to a boil. Remove from heat. Add tea bags; let stand 15 minutes. Remove tea bags. Stir in remaining 1 quart cold water. Add remaining ingredients; stir until well blended. Cover and refrigerate until well chilled. To serve, pour tea over prepared ice cubes.

Yield: about ten 6-ounce servings

1 serving (6 ounces tea):
32 calories, 0.1 gram fat, 0.5 gram protein, 8.3 grams carbohydrate

SINLESS BROWNIES

1 1/2 cups sugar
1 cup all-purpose flour
1/3 cup cocoa
1/2 teaspoon baking powder
1/4 teaspoon salt
1/4 cup egg substitute
1/4 cup water
1 egg white
2 tablespoons reduced-calorie margarine, softened
1 tablespoon vanilla extract
Vegetable cooking spray

Preheat oven to 350 degrees. In a medium bowl, combine sugar, flour, cocoa, baking powder, and salt. Add egg substitute, water, egg white, margarine, and vanilla; stir until well blended. Spoon batter into an 8-inch square baking pan sprayed with cooking spray. Bake 25 to 30 minutes or until dry on top and set in center. Cut into 2-inch squares.
Yield: about 16 brownies

1 serving (one 2-inch square brownie): 97 calories, 1.0 gram fat, 1.5 grams protein, 22.3 grams carbohydrate

PRALINE COFFEE

2 quarts brewed coffee
3 cans (12 ounces each) evaporated skimmed milk
1/2 cup firmly packed brown sugar
3 cups fat-free vanilla ice cream, softened
1 cup vodka
1 tablespoon vanilla extract
2 teaspoons maple flavoring

In a Dutch oven, combine coffee, milk, and sugar. Stirring occasionally, cook over medium-high heat until mixture begins to boil; remove from heat. Stir in ice cream, vodka, vanilla, and maple flavoring. Serve hot.
Yield: about twenty 6-ounce servings

1 serving (6 ounces coffee): 113 calories, 0.1 gram fat, 5.1 grams protein, 16.2 grams carbohydrate

Fat-free vanilla ice cream and vodka lend holiday appeal to luscious Praline Coffee, and Sinless Brownies are moist, chewy treats. Mandarin oranges and marmalade add a colorful touch to miniature low-fat Orange Cheesecakes.

ORANGE CHEESECAKES

12 vanilla wafers
1 1/2 cups (12 ounces) fat-free cream cheese, softened
1 cup fat-free sour cream
1/2 cup sugar
1/2 cup egg substitute
2 tablespoons all-purpose flour
2 teaspoons orange extract
1 can (11 ounces) mandarin oranges, well drained
2 tablespoons orange marmalade

Preheat oven to 350 degrees. Place 1 vanilla wafer into bottom of each paper-lined cup of a muffin pan. In a medium bowl, beat cream cheese until fluffy. Add sour cream, sugar, egg substitute, flour, and orange extract; beat until smooth. Spoon cheese mixture over vanilla wafers, filling each cup full. Bake 18 minutes. Turn oven off and leave in oven 2 minutes. Leaving oven door ajar, leave in oven 15 minutes longer. Cool completely in pan.

In a small bowl, combine oranges and marmalade. Spoon orange mixture on top of each cheesecake. Loosely cover and store in refrigerator. Serve chilled.
Yield: 1 dozen cheesecakes

1 serving (1 cheesecake): 110 calories, 0.6 gram fat, 6.6 grams protein, 18.2 grams carbohydrate

For a light and luscious dessert, try Baked Honey Fruit. Served with a dollop of whipped topping, Spiced Irish Coffee is a spirited holiday beverage — and a great accompaniment to Blueberry Tea Buns. These wholesome scone-like treats are bursting with fruit.

BAKED HONEY FRUIT

1 can (20 ounces) pineapple chunks in juice
2 tablespoons cornstarch
1 jar (6 ounces) maraschino cherries, drained
1 1/2 cups coarsely chopped orange sections
1 1/2 cups coarsely chopped grapefruit sections
1/3 cup honey
4 fresh mint leaves, chopped
Fresh mint leaves to garnish

Preheat oven to 375 degrees. Reserving juice, drain pineapple. In a small bowl, dissolve cornstarch in reserved pineapple juice. In a medium bowl, combine pineapple, cherries, orange, grapefruit, honey, and chopped mint leaves. Stir in cornstarch mixture. Pour fruit mixture into a 9-inch square baking dish. Bake 1 hour or until mixture is thick and bubbly. Garnish each serving with mint leaves. Serve warm.
Yield: about 9 servings

1 serving (1/2 cup): 128 calories, 0.2 gram fat, 0.8 gram protein, 33.9 grams carbohydrate

BLUEBERRY TEA BUNS

1/3 cup plus 1 tablespoon sugar, divided
1 3/4 cups all-purpose flour
1 teaspoon ground cinnamon
1 teaspoon baking soda
1/2 teaspoon salt
1 can (8 ounces) crushed pineapple in juice, lightly drained
1/4 cup skim milk
3 tablespoons vegetable oil
1/4 cup egg substitute
1 1/2 cups frozen blueberries (do not thaw)
Vegetable cooking spray

Preheat oven to 400 degrees. In a medium bowl, combine 1/3 cup sugar, flour, cinnamon, baking soda, and salt; make a well in center of mixture. Combine pineapple, milk, oil, and egg substitute; add to dry ingredients. Stir just until dry ingredients are moistened. Gently stir in blueberries. Drop batter by heaping tablespoonfuls onto a baking sheet sprayed with cooking spray. Sprinkle remaining 1 tablespoon sugar over batter. Bake 12 to 15 minutes or until golden brown. Serve warm.
Yield: about 24 muffins

1 serving (1 muffin): 75 calories, 2.0 grams fat, 1.4 grams protein, 13.1 grams carbohydrate

SPICED IRISH COFFEE

1/3 cup plus 2 tablespoons sugar, divided
1/4 teaspoon ground cinnamon
2 cups skim milk
2 cinnamon sticks
1 whole nutmeg, crushed
2 1/2 quarts hot, strongly brewed coffee
3 tablespoons fat-free non-dairy powdered creamer
2/3 cup Irish whiskey
Fat-free frozen whipped topping, thawed to garnish

In a small bowl, combine 2 tablespoons sugar and ground cinnamon; set aside. Combine remaining 1/3 cup sugar, milk, cinnamon sticks, and nutmeg in a Dutch oven. Cook over medium-low heat, stirring until sugar dissolves. Stir in coffee and creamer. Cover and heat 5 minutes to allow flavors to blend. Remove from heat; strain and discard cinnamon sticks and nutmeg. Stir in Irish whiskey. Pour into 8-ounce Irish coffee glasses. Garnish each serving with 1 tablespoon whipped topping and sprinkle with sugar-cinnamon mixture. Serve immediately.
Yield: about 12 cups coffee

1 serving (8 ounces): 91 calories, 0.1 gram fat, 1.6 grams protein, 13.5 grams carbohydrate

Made with half the fat of traditional cinnamon rolls, Chocolate-Cinnamon Rolls are delicious served warm from the oven. Diet Crispy Cookies (not shown) are another light and satisfying way of pleasing even the sweetest tooth!

CHOCOLATE-CINNAMON ROLLS

DOUGH
1	package quick-acting dry yeast
1	cup warm water
2³/4	cups all-purpose flour
1/2	cup cocoa
1/2	cup sugar
1	teaspoon salt
1/4	cup egg substitute
1 1/2	tablespoons vegetable oil
	Vegetable cooking spray

FILLING
3	tablespoons sugar, divided
4	teaspoons ground cinnamon, divided
3	tablespoons reduced-calorie margarine, divided
1 1/3	cups reduced-fat chocolate chips, divided
	Vegetable cooking spray

GLAZE
1/2	cup confectioners sugar
2	teaspoons water

For dough, dissolve yeast in 1 cup warm water in a small bowl. In a large bowl, combine flour, cocoa, sugar, and salt. Add egg substitute, oil, and yeast mixture to dry ingredients; stir until a soft dough forms. Turn onto a lightly floured surface and knead about 3 minutes or until dough becomes smooth and elastic. Place in a large bowl sprayed with cooking spray, turning once to coat top of dough. Cover and let rise in a warm place (80 to 85 degrees) 1 hour or until almost doubled in size.

For filling, combine 1 1/2 tablespoons sugar and 2 teaspoons cinnamon in a small bowl; set aside. Turn dough onto a lightly floured surface and punch down. Divide dough in half. Roll out half of dough to a 10 x 16-inch rectangle. Spread 1 1/2 tablespoons margarine over dough; sprinkle sugar mixture and 2/3 cup chocolate chips over dough. Beginning at 1 long edge, roll up tightly. Cut into 1-inch-wide slices and place, cut side down, in a lightly sprayed 8-inch square baking dish. Repeat with remaining ingredients. Lightly spray tops of dough with cooking spray, cover, and let rise in a warm place 1 hour or until almost doubled in size.

Preheat oven to 375 degrees. Bake 18 to 23 minutes.

For glaze, combine confectioners sugar and water in a small bowl; stir until smooth. Drizzle over warm rolls; serve warm.

Yield: 32 cinnamon rolls

1 serving (1 roll): 120 calories, 4.1 grams fat, 1.7 grams protein, 22.4 grams carbohydrate

DIET CRISPY COOKIES

1	small orange
1	cup boiling water
2	eggs
3/4	cup confectioners sugar
1	teaspoon grated orange zest
2/3	cup all-purpose flour
1/8	teaspoon salt
3/4	cup crispy rice cereal

Preheat oven to 350 degrees. Line a baking sheet with aluminum foil. Carefully peel orange, making sure not to leave any white pith on peel. Cut peel into very thin 1-inch-long strips. Place strips in a small bowl and pour boiling water into bowl. Let sit 5 minutes; drain.

In a medium bowl, combine eggs, confectioners sugar, and zest. Beat until well blended. In a small bowl, combine flour and salt; stir into egg mixture. Stir in cereal. Drop teaspoonfuls of dough onto prepared baking sheet; spread into circles. Top each with a few strips of orange peel. Bake 8 to 10 minutes or until edges are lightly browned. Cool cookies on foil; carefully peel off foil. Store in an airtight container.

Yield: about 2 1/2 dozen cookies

1 serving (1 cookie): 31 calories, 0.4 gram fat, 0.8 gram protein, 6.1 grams carbohydrate

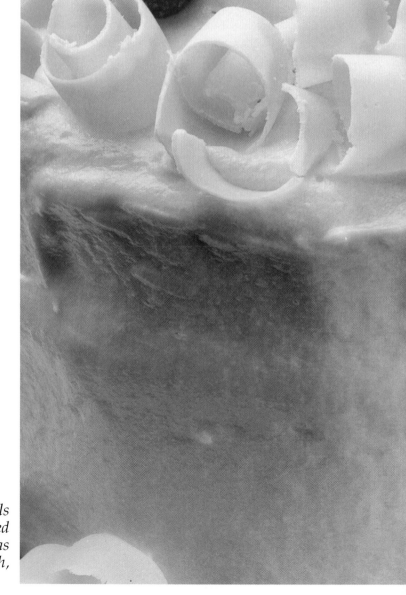

DELIGHTFUL DESSERTS

Skipping dessert is never an option during the Christmas season! That's why this collection of tantalizing recipes contains so many wonderful choices. You can indulge anyone's sweet-tooth, whether you're hosting a holiday get-together or just looking for that perfect finish to a festive meal. You'll also find some tempting treats for satisfying those inevitable chocolate cravings. So go ahead — there's never been a better time to splurge!

Crowned with white chocolate curls and fresh cranberries sprinkled with red sugar, this delectable Red Christmas Cake (recipe on page 104) has a rich, chocolaty flavor.

RED CHRISTMAS CAKE

(Shown on pages 102 and 103)

CAKE

- $2/3$ cup butter or margarine, softened
- $1 2/3$ cups sugar
- 2 eggs, separated
- 1 bottle (1 ounce) red liquid food coloring
- $2 1/4$ cups sifted cake flour
- $1/4$ cup cocoa
- 1 teaspoon baking soda
- $3/4$ teaspoon salt
- 1 cup plus 2 tablespoons buttermilk
- 2 teaspoons white vinegar
- 2 tablespoons vanilla extract

ICING

- 3 ounces white baking chocolate
- 11 ounces cream cheese, softened
- $1/3$ cup chilled butter, cut into pieces
- 1 teaspoon vanilla extract
- $2 1/2$ cups confectioners sugar

DECORATIONS

- 3 ounces white baking chocolate
- 2 teaspoons meringue powder **or** egg-white powder
- 2 tablespoons water
  Fresh cranberries
  Red decorating sugar

Preheat oven to 350 degrees. For cake, grease three 8-inch round cake pans and line bottoms with waxed paper. In a large bowl, cream butter and sugar until fluffy. Add egg yolks and food coloring; beat until well blended. In a medium bowl, combine cake flour, cocoa, baking soda, and salt. In a small bowl, combine buttermilk and vinegar. Alternately beat dry ingredients and buttermilk mixture into creamed mixture until smooth. Stir in vanilla. Beat egg whites in a small bowl until stiff peaks form; fold into batter. Pour batter into prepared pans. Bake 20 to 30 minutes or until a toothpick inserted in center of cake comes out clean. Cool in pans 10 minutes. Remove from pans and cool on a wire rack.

For icing, microwave white chocolate in a microwave-safe dish on medium-high power (80%) $1 1/2$ to $2 1/2$ minutes or until chocolate softens, stirring after

each minute; stir until melted. In a medium bowl, beat cream cheese and butter until fluffy. Add melted chocolate and vanilla; beat until smooth. Beat in confectioners sugar until well blended. Spread icing between layers and over top and sides of cake. Place in an airtight container in refrigerator until ready to serve.

For decorations, melt white chocolate and pour into a $2 1/4$ x 4-inch loaf pan. Chill just until firm. Remove chocolate from pan. See Making Chocolate Curls, page 119, to make curls; chill curls.

To sugar cranberries, beat meringue powder and water in a small bowl until foamy. Dip cranberries into mixture. Place on a wire rack. Sprinkle red decorating sugar over wet cranberries; allow to dry. Garnish cake with white chocolate curls and sugared cranberries.

Yield: about 16 servings

Fast and easy to make, our Chocolate-Covered Cherry Pie is a tasty frozen concoction served in a ready-made chocolate crust. Maraschino cherries and chocolate sprinkles top off the cool confection.

CHOCOLATE-COVERED CHERRY PIE

- 1 box (8 ounces) chocolate-covered cherries, quartered
- 1 quart vanilla ice cream, softened
- 1 9-inch purchased chocolate crumb pie crust
- 8 maraschino cherries with stems (undrained) and chocolate sprinkles to garnish

In a medium bowl, stir chocolate-covered cherries into ice cream. Spoon ice cream mixture into crust. Dip maraschino cherries in chocolate sprinkles and place on pie to garnish. Add additional chocolate sprinkles to pie as desired. Place in freezer until firm.

Yield: about 8 servings

FUDGE BROWNIE CAKE

CAKE

- 1½ cups butter or margarine
- 6 ounces unsweetened baking chocolate, chopped
- 6 eggs
- 1½ teaspoons vanilla extract
- 3 cups sugar
- 1¾ cups all-purpose flour
- 2 cups chopped pecans

ICING

- 3¾ cups confectioners sugar, divided
- ½ cup butter or margarine
- 6 tablespoons milk
- 3 tablespoons cocoa
- 1 teaspoon vanilla extract
- 1 cup finely chopped pecans
- 2 cups whipping cream
  Chocolate curls to garnish

Preheat oven to 325 degrees. For cake, grease three 8-inch round cake pans. Line bottoms of pans with waxed paper; grease waxed paper. Place butter and chocolate in the top of a double boiler over simmering water. Stirring frequently, heat just until mixture melts. Remove from heat. In a large bowl, beat eggs and vanilla until blended. Stirring constantly, gradually add melted chocolate mixture to egg mixture. In a medium bowl, combine sugar and flour. Gradually stir dry ingredients into chocolate mixture just until blended. Stir in pecans. Spread batter into prepared pans. Bake 25 to 30 minutes or until cake is firm to touch. Cool in pans on a wire rack.

For icing, place 3½ cups confectioners sugar in a large bowl. In a heavy small saucepan, combine butter, milk, and cocoa. Stirring constantly, cook over medium heat until butter melts. Remove from heat; stir in vanilla. Pour chocolate mixture over confectioners sugar; stir until smooth. Stir in pecans. Let icing cool about 15 minutes or until firm enough to spread. Spread icing between layers and on top of cake.

In a medium bowl, beat whipping cream until soft peaks form.

Scrumptiously rich, three-layer Fudge Brownie Cake is enhanced with a yummy frosting and sweetened whipped cream. Whether served hot or cold, Raspberry Coffee is a sweet indulgence.

Gradually adding remaining ¼ cup confectioners sugar, beat until stiff peaks form. Ice sides and top edge of cake with whipped cream. Store in an airtight container in refrigerator. To serve, garnish with chocolate curls.
Yield: about 16 servings

RASPBERRY COFFEE

- 1 cup half and half
- ⅔ cup sugar
- 1 quart hot, strongly brewed raspberry-flavored coffee

For hot coffee, place half and half and sugar in a small saucepan over medium-low heat. Stirring frequently, heat about 10 minutes or until hot. Combine coffee and half and half mixture in a 1½-quart heatproof container; serve hot.

For iced coffee, combine coffee and sugar in a 1½-quart heatproof container. Stir until sugar dissolves; cover and chill. To serve, stir half and half into coffee mixture; serve over ice.
Yield: about 5 cups coffee

A wreath of candied cherries makes a festive statement atop this moist Cherry Spice Cake.

CHERRY SPICE CAKE

CAKE

- 1/2 cup butter or margarine, softened
- 2 cups sugar
- 2 eggs
- 2 1/2 cups all-purpose flour
- 1 1/2 teaspoons baking soda
- 1 1/2 teaspoons ground nutmeg
- 1 teaspoon ground cinnamon
- 1/2 teaspoon ground cloves
- 1/2 teaspoon ground allspice
- 1 1/2 cups cherry pie filling

FROSTING

- 2 packages (8 ounces each) cream cheese, softened
- 1 cup butter or margarine, softened
- 3 tablespoons milk
- 1 tablespoon vanilla extract
- 8 cups confectioners sugar
  Red and green candied cherries to decorate

Preheat oven to 350 degrees. For cake, cream butter and sugar in a large bowl until fluffy. Add eggs, 1 at a time, beating well after each addition. In a medium bowl, combine flour, baking soda, nutmeg, cinnamon, cloves, and allspice. Process pie filling in a food processor until cherries are coarsely chopped. Alternately add dry ingredients and cherries to creamed mixture, beating until well blended. Pour batter into 3 greased and floured 9-inch round cake pans. Bake 30 to 35 minutes or until a toothpick inserted in center of cake comes out clean. Cool in pans 10 minutes. Remove from pans and cool completely on a wire rack.

For frosting, beat cream cheese, butter, milk, and vanilla until fluffy. Gradually adding confectioners sugar, beat until smooth. Spread frosting between layers and on top and sides of cake. Cut cherries in half and decorate top of cake with wreath design. Spoon remaining icing into a pastry bag fitted with a star tip. Pipe stars around top and bottom of cake. Cover and store in an airtight container in refrigerator. Serve at room temperature.

Yield: about 20 servings

Almond Rosettes are melt-in-your-mouth morsels! Whipping cream and ice cream give liqueur-laced Creamy Coffee Punch its frothiness.

ALMOND ROSETTES

- 1 cup butter or margarine, softened
- 1 cup sugar
- 1 egg
- 3 tablespoons milk
- 1 teaspoon almond extract
- 2 1/2 cups all-purpose flour
- 1 teaspoon baking powder
  Sliced almonds to decorate

Preheat oven to 350 degrees. In a large bowl, cream butter and sugar until fluffy. Add egg, milk, and almond extract; beat until smooth. In a medium bowl, combine flour and baking powder. Add dry ingredients to creamed mixture; stir until a soft dough forms. Transfer about one-third of dough into a pastry bag fitted with a large open star tip. Pipe 2-inch-diameter rosettes onto a lightly greased baking sheet. Press an almond slice in center of each cookie. Bake 8 to 11 minutes or until bottoms are lightly browned. Transfer cookies to a wire rack to cool. Repeat with remaining dough. Store in an airtight container.

Yield: about 3 1/2 dozen cookies

CREAMY COFFEE PUNCH

- 2 quarts hot, strongly brewed coffee
- 3 tablespoons sugar
- 2 teaspoons vanilla extract
- 2 cups coffee-flavored liqueur
- 1 quart vanilla ice cream, softened
- 2 cups whipping cream, whipped

Place coffee in a 3-quart heatproof container. Add sugar and vanilla; stir until sugar dissolves. Allow mixture to cool. Stir in liqueur; cover and chill.

To serve, pour chilled coffee mixture into a punch bowl. Stir in ice cream. Fold in whipped cream. Serve immediately.

Yield: about 16 cups punch

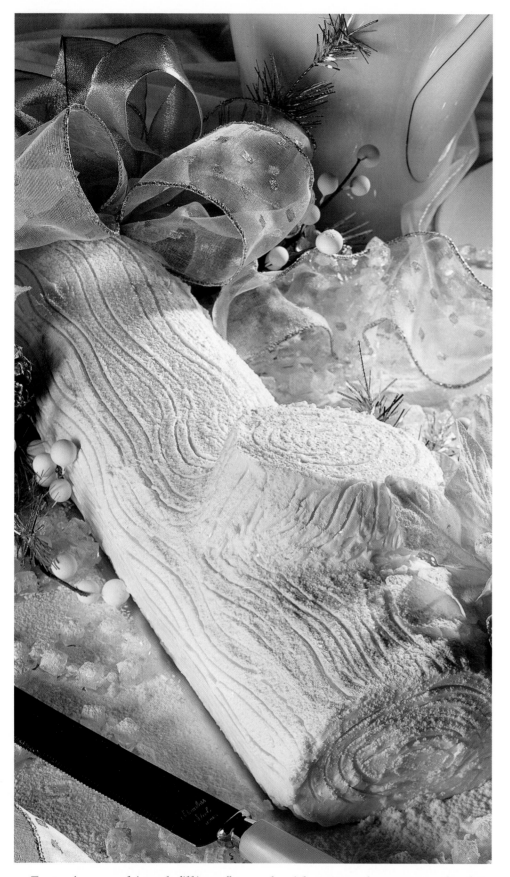

Featuring a whipped filling flavored with crème de cacao and white baking chocolate, our White Chocolate Yule Log is so delicious that not even a crumb will be left! The iced cake is dusted with confectioners sugar and edible glitter "snow" for an enchanting finish.

WHITE CHOCOLATE YULE LOG

CAKE
- 5 eggs, separated
- $2/3$ cup granulated sugar, divided
- 2 tablespoons butter or margarine, melted
- $1^1/2$ teaspoons vanilla extract
- $3/4$ cup sifted cake flour
- $1^1/4$ teaspoons baking powder
- $1/4$ teaspoon salt
- 2 tablespoons confectioners sugar

FILLING
- 3 tablespoons butter
- 1 egg yolk
- $2/3$ cup plus 1 tablespoon whipping cream, divided
- 1 tablespoon white crème de cacao
- 1 ounce white baking chocolate
- 1 tablespoon confectioners sugar

ICING
- $1/4$ cup milk
- 2 ounces white baking chocolate
- 1 teaspoon vanilla extract
- $3/4$ cup chilled butter, cut into pieces
- 1 cup confectioners sugar
  Confectioners sugar, white edible glitter, bows, and artificial decorations to decorate

Preheat oven to 350 degrees. For cake, grease a $10^1/2$ x $15^1/2$-inch jellyroll pan. Line bottom of pan with waxed paper; grease waxed paper. In a large bowl, beat egg yolks until thick. Add $1/3$ cup granulated sugar; beat until well blended. Beat in melted butter and vanilla. In another large bowl, beat egg whites until foamy. Gradually add remaining $1/3$ cup granulated sugar; beat until stiff peaks form. Fold egg white mixture into egg yolk mixture. In a small bowl, combine cake flour, baking powder, and salt. Sift about one-fourth of flour mixture at a time over egg mixture, folding in flour after each addition until mixture is well blended. Pour batter into prepared pan. Bake 11 to

14 minutes or until toothpick inserted in center of cake comes out clean. Sift confectioners sugar onto a towel. Loosen edges of cake and immediately invert onto towel. Remove waxed paper from cake. Beginning with 1 long edge, roll cake in towel and allow to cool.

For filling, combine butter, egg yolk, and 1 tablespoon whipping cream in a heavy small saucepan. Stirring constantly, cook over low heat about 8 minutes or until mixture thickens. Remove from heat. Stir in crème de cacao and white chocolate; stir until chocolate melts. Transfer chocolate mixture to a medium bowl; cool about 30 minutes.

In another medium bowl, beat remaining 2/3 cup whipping cream until soft peaks form. Add confectioners sugar; beat until stiff peaks form. Fold into chocolate mixture. Unroll cake and spread filling over cake. Roll up cake. Place on a serving plate; cover and chill while making icing.

For icing, place milk and white chocolate in a small microwave-safe bowl. Microwave on medium power (50%) 1 1/2 minutes or until chocolate softens, stirring every 30 seconds. Stir until chocolate melts. Stir in vanilla. Cool 30 minutes or until chocolate mixture reaches room temperature. In a medium bowl, beat butter and confectioners sugar until smooth and creamy. Gradually add chocolate mixture; beat until well blended. Cut a 1-inch slice from one end of cake roll. Place on top of "log" to form "knot." Spread icing over cake roll. Chill cake 5 minutes to let icing harden slightly. Use tines of a fork to form "bark" lines in icing. Sift confectioners sugar and sprinkle glitter over cake for "snow." Decorate cake with bows and artificial decorations.

Yield: about 16 servings

For a simple yet elegant dessert, try Meringue Snowballs in Custard. The poached meringue dollops are served in a sauce of creamy vanilla custard.

MERINGUE SNOWBALLS IN CUSTARD

6	egg yolks
2/3	cup plus 1/4 cup sugar, divided
6 1/4	cups milk, divided
1 1/2	teaspoons vanilla extract
2	egg whites
1/4	teaspoon cream of tartar

In a small bowl, beat egg yolks and 2/3 cup sugar until well blended. Combine egg yolk mixture and 4 cups milk in the top of a double boiler over simmering water. Stirring constantly, cook about 30 minutes or until mixture coats the back of a spoon. Stir in vanilla. Pour custard into a 9 x 13-inch serving dish. Place plastic wrap directly on surface of custard; chill.

Place remaining 2 1/4 cups milk in a heavy large skillet over medium-low heat. In a medium bowl, beat egg whites until foamy. Gradually add remaining 1/4 cup sugar and cream of tartar; beat until stiff peaks form. When milk is almost to a simmer, use 2 spoons to form and drop rounded tablespoonfuls of meringue into milk. Poach meringues about 4 minutes, turning once during cooking (meringues should be firm to touch). With a slotted spoon, remove meringues from milk; transfer to paper towels to drain. Place meringues on custard. Chill completely before serving.

Yield: about 12 servings

The ultimate treat for a chocoholic, Death by Chocolate Cake features layers of moist cake and creamy filling topped with yummy fudge frosting and lots of chocolate curls.

DEATH BY CHOCOLATE CAKE

CAKE
- 1 package (18¼ ounces) devil's food cake mix without pudding in the mix
- 1 package (3.9 ounces) chocolate fudge instant pudding mix
- 3 eggs
- 1¼ cups water
- ½ cup vegetable oil
- 1½ cups semisweet chocolate chips

FILLING
- 1 can (20 ounces) evaporated milk, divided
- 1½ cups sugar
- 5 tablespoons all-purpose flour
- 4 egg yolks
- 2 tablespoons butter or margarine, melted
- 1 teaspoon vanilla extract
- ½ teaspoon almond extract
- 2 ounces semisweet baking chocolate

FROSTING
- ½ cup butter or margarine
- 6 tablespoons sour cream
- ¼ cup cocoa
- 3½ cups confectioners sugar
- 1 teaspoon vanilla extract
- 1 cup chopped pecans
- 1 package (12 ounces) semisweet chocolate chips for chocolate curls

Preheat oven to 350 degrees. For cake, combine cake mix, pudding mix, eggs, water, and oil in a large bowl. Using low speed of an electric mixer, beat until moistened. Increase speed of mixer to medium and beat 2 minutes. Stir in chocolate chips. Pour batter into 2 greased and floured 9-inch round cake pans. Bake 30 to 35 minutes or until cake begins to pull away from sides of pan and springs back when lightly pressed. Cool in pans 10 minutes; invert onto a wire rack to cool completely. Slice each layer in half horizontally. Separate layers with waxed paper and wrap in plastic wrap. Freeze layers until firm.

For filling, combine 1/4 cup evaporated milk, sugar, flour, egg yolks, butter, and extracts in a small bowl; set aside. Combine chocolate and remaining evaporated milk in a medium saucepan. Stirring constantly, cook over medium heat until chocolate melts. Pour sugar mixture into chocolate mixture. Stirring constantly, bring to a boil; boil 3 to 4 minutes or until thickened. Remove from heat. Cover and refrigerate until well chilled.

Place 1 layer of cake on serving plate. Spread one-third of filling evenly over cake layer. Repeat with remaining filling and second and third cake layers. Place remaining cake layer on top. Cover and refrigerate until ready to frost.

For frosting, combine butter, sour cream, and cocoa in a large saucepan. Stirring occasionally, bring to a boil over medium heat. Remove from heat. Add confectioners sugar and vanilla; beat until smooth. Spread warm frosting on top and sides of cake. Press pecans onto sides of cake. Allow frosting to cool completely.

For chocolate curls, melt chocolate chips in a small saucepan over low heat, stirring constantly. Pour onto a baking sheet, spreading chocolate to form an 8 x 11-inch rectangle. Refrigerate until set but not firm.

To make curls, pull a chocolate curler or vegetable peeler across surface of chocolate (curls will break if chocolate is too firm). Remelt and cool chocolate as necessary to form desired number of curls. Arrange curls on top of cake. Store cake in an airtight container in refrigerator.

Yield: about 20 servings

BUTTERMILK PECAN PIES

CRUST
- 1/2 cup butter or margarine, softened
- 1 package (3 ounces) cream cheese, softened
- 1 cup plus 1 tablespoon all-purpose flour

Rosemary Tea has a refreshing, distinctive flavor. Cream cheese pastry and a rich, sweet filling make Buttermilk Pecan Pies extra special.

FILLING
- 3/4 cup sugar
- 1 egg
- 1/3 cup buttermilk
- 3 tablespoons butter or margarine, melted
- 1 tablespoon all-purpose flour
- 1/4 teaspoon salt
- 3/4 cup chopped pecans

For crust, beat butter and cream cheese in a medium bowl until smooth; stir in flour. Shape dough into twenty-four 1-inch balls. Press balls of dough into bottoms and up sides of greased cups of miniature muffin pans.

Preheat oven to 350 degrees. For filling, beat sugar and egg in a medium bowl. Add buttermilk, melted butter, flour, and salt; beat until smooth. Stir in pecans. Spoon filling into crusts, filling each cup. Bake 30 to 35 minutes or until golden brown. Cool in pans 5 minutes. Transfer to a wire rack to cool completely. Store in an airtight container.

Yield: 2 dozen pies

ROSEMARY TEA

- 1/2 cup tea leaves
- 1 tablespoon dried rosemary leaves

Process tea leaves and rosemary in a food processor until finely ground. Store in an airtight container.

To brew tea, place 1 teaspoon tea for each 8 ounces of water in a warm teapot. Bring water to a rolling boil and pour over tea. Steep tea 5 minutes; strain. Serve hot or over ice.

Yield: about 1/3 cup tea leaves

Buttery banana and streusel toppings make Banana Crumb Cake a moist treat. Guests will love pairing the cake with Caramel Mocha — a smooth after-dinner beverage flavored with caramel ice cream topping and chocolate syrup.

BANANA CRUMB CAKE

BANANA TOPPING
- 1/2 cup firmly packed brown sugar
- 2 teaspoons cornstarch
- 1/2 cup water
- 2 tablespoons butter or margarine
- 2 bananas, sliced

CRUMB MIXTURE
- 1 cup all-purpose flour
- 2/3 cup firmly packed brown sugar
- 3/4 teaspoon ground cinnamon
- 1/2 cup chilled butter or margarine

CAKE
- 3/4 cup butter or margarine, softened
- 1 1/4 cups sugar
- 2 eggs
- 2 teaspoons vanilla extract
- 2 cups all-purpose flour
- 1 teaspoon baking powder
- 1/2 teaspoon baking soda
- 3/4 cup buttermilk

For banana topping, combine brown sugar and cornstarch in a heavy small saucepan. Stirring constantly over medium-high heat, gradually add water. Bring mixture to a boil; cook about 1 minute or until mixture begins to thicken. Add butter; stir until butter melts. Remove from heat. Stir in banana slices; set aside.

For crumb mixture, combine flour, brown sugar, and cinnamon in a medium bowl. With a pastry blender or 2 forks, cut in butter until mixture resembles very coarse crumbs; set aside.

Preheat oven to 350 degrees. For cake, cream butter and sugar in a large bowl until fluffy. Add eggs; beat until smooth. Stir in vanilla. In a medium bowl, combine flour, baking powder, and baking soda. Alternately add dry ingredients and buttermilk to creamed mixture; beat until well blended. Spread batter in a greased 10-inch springform pan. Spoon banana topping over batter. Sprinkle crumb mixture over topping. Bake 50 to 60 minutes or until top is golden brown and a toothpick inserted in center of cake comes out clean. Cool cake in pan 30 minutes. Remove sides of pan; serve warm.
Yield: about 12 servings

CARAMEL MOCHA

- 1 can (14 ounces) sweetened condensed milk
- 1 container (12 ounces) caramel ice cream topping
- 1/2 cup chocolate-flavored syrup
- 2 1/2 quarts hot, strongly brewed coffee (we used espresso roast coffee)

In a small Dutch oven, combine sweetened condensed milk, caramel topping, and chocolate syrup. Stirring constantly, cook over medium-low heat about 8 minutes or until mixture is well blended and hot. Add coffee; stir until blended. Serve hot.
Yield: about 12 cups coffee

NUTTY FUDGE PIE

- 1 cup sugar
- 1/2 cup butter or margarine, melted
- 1/2 cup all-purpose flour
- 1/2 cup chopped pecans
- 2 eggs
- 3 tablespoons cocoa
- 1 teaspoon vanilla extract
  Ice cream and chopped pecans to serve

(**Note:** Recipe was tested in a 750-watt microwave.) In a medium bowl, combine sugar, butter, flour, pecans, eggs, cocoa, and vanilla; beat until well blended. Pour batter into a greased 9-inch microwave-safe pie plate. Microwave on medium power (60%) 10 to 12 minutes or until almost set in center (do not overbake). Serve warm with ice cream and pecans.
Yield: about 8 servings

SPICED COFFEE MIX

- 1 cup instant coffee granules
- 2/3 cup firmly packed brown sugar
- 2 teaspoons ground cinnamon
  Cinnamon sticks to garnish

Process coffee granules, brown sugar, and cinnamon in a food processor until well blended. Store in an airtight container.

To serve, stir 1 teaspoon coffee into 6 ounces hot water. Garnish with a cinnamon stick.
Yield: about 1 1/2 cups coffee mix

When you need a luscious dessert for unexpected guests, try microwavable Nutty Fudge Pie, and you'll have a sweet treat in minutes. A warming mug of Spiced Coffee is just seconds away with a store of simple dry ingredients.

Loaded with cinnamon, nutmeg, and fruit, Apple Streusel Pie is so tasty that no one will guess it's low-fat! A crunchy oat topping adds the finishing touch.

APPLE STREUSEL PIE

CRUST
- ³/₄ cup sifted cake flour
- ¹/₂ teaspoon sugar
- ¹/₈ teaspoon salt
- ¹/₈ teaspoon baking powder
- 2 tablespoons chilled margarine (not reduced-calorie), cut into pieces
- 2 tablespoons cold water
  Vegetable cooking spray

FILLING
- ³/₄ cup sugar
- 2 tablespoons all-purpose flour
- 1 teaspoon ground cinnamon
- ¹/₄ teaspoon ground nutmeg
- 5 cups peeled, cored, and sliced baking apples (about 4 large apples)

TOPPING
- ¹/₃ cup quick-cooking oats
- 2 tablespoons sugar
- 2 tablespoons all-purpose flour
- 2 tablespoons chilled reduced-calorie margarine, cut into pieces

Preheat oven to 400 degrees. For crust, combine cake flour, sugar, salt, and baking powder in a small bowl. Using a pastry blender or 2 knives, cut in margarine until mixture resembles coarse meal. Sprinkle with water; stir with a fork until moistened. Shape dough into a ball and place between 2 sheets of plastic wrap. Roll out dough into a 12-inch circle. Remove top sheet of plastic wrap. Invert dough into a 9-inch pie plate sprayed with cooking spray. Remove remaining sheet of plastic wrap. Fold edges of dough under and flute. Prick bottom of crust with a fork. Bake 8 minutes; set aside.

Reduce oven temperature to 375 degrees. For filling, combine sugar, flour, cinnamon, and nutmeg in a large bowl. Stir in apples. Spoon apple mixture into crust. Bake 25 minutes.

For topping, combine oats, sugar, and flour in a small bowl; cut in margarine with a fork until mixture is crumbly. Sprinkle over pie; bake 45 to 55 minutes or until topping is lightly browned. Cool 1 hour before serving.

Yield: 8 servings

1 serving: 236 calories, 4.7 grams fat, 1.9 grams protein, 46.1 grams carbohydrate

CHRISTMAS STOCKING COOKIES

COOKIES
- 1/2 cup butter or margarine, softened
- 1/2 cup granulated sugar
- 1/2 cup firmly packed brown sugar
- 1 egg
- 1 teaspoon vanilla extract
- 1 1/2 cups all-purpose flour
- 1/2 teaspoon baking powder
- 1/2 teaspoon ground cinnamon
- 1/4 teaspoon salt

GLAZE
- 3 cups confectioners sugar
- 1/4 cup plus 1 teaspoon milk
- 1 teaspoon clear vanilla extract

ROYAL ICING
- 1 cup confectioners sugar
- 1 tablespoon plus 1 teaspoon water
- 2 teaspoons meringue powder
- 1/2 teaspoon clear vanilla extract
  Yellow, red, and green paste food coloring

For cookies, cream butter and sugars in a large bowl until fluffy. Add egg and vanilla; beat until smooth. In a small bowl, combine flour, baking powder, cinnamon, and salt. Add dry ingredients to creamed mixture; stir until a soft dough forms. Divide dough in half. Wrap in plastic wrap and chill 2 hours.

Preheat oven to 375 degrees. On a lightly floured surface, use a floured rolling pin to roll out half of dough to 1/4-inch thickness. Use a 2 1/2 x 4 3/4-inch stocking-shaped cookie cutter to cut out cookies. Transfer to an ungreased baking sheet. Bake 8 to 10 minutes or until edges are lightly browned. Transfer cookies to a wire rack to cool. Repeat for remaining dough.

For glaze, combine confectioners sugar, milk, and vanilla in a medium bowl; stir until smooth. Spread glaze on tops of cookies. Allow glaze to harden.

Guests will want to fill up on these buttery little cookies! Christmas Stocking Cookies are decorated with glaze and colorful piped-on royal icing, then personalized.

For royal icing, beat confectioners sugar, water, meringue powder, and vanilla in a medium bowl at high speed of an electric mixer 7 to 10 minutes or until stiff. Tint 1/4 cup icing yellow. Divide remaining icing in half and tint red and green. Spoon icings into pastry bags. Using a small round tip, pipe ruffle, name, and outline of toe and heel on each stocking. Using a very small round tip, pipe plaid patterns on each stocking. Allow icing to harden. Store cookies in a single layer in an airtight container. **Yield:** about 1 1/4 dozen cookies

Bananas, chocolate, and pecans are nestled in a graham cracker crust to create this delectable Banana-Pecan Tart.

BANANA-PECAN TART

CRUST

1³/₄ cups graham cracker crumbs
¹/₃ cup all-purpose flour
¹/₃ cup sugar
6 tablespoons butter or margarine, melted

FILLING

3 ripe bananas, sliced
¹/₂ cup sugar
¹/₄ cup light corn syrup
2 eggs
¹/₄ cup butter or margarine, melted
1 tablespoon vanilla extract
1 teaspoon rum flavoring
2 ounces semisweet baking chocolate, melted

1¹/₂ cups chopped pecans
1 package (6 ounces) semisweet chocolate chips, divided

For crust, combine graham cracker crumbs, flour, sugar, and melted butter in a medium bowl until well blended. Press into bottom and up sides of a greased 8 x 11-inch tart pan with removable bottom; set aside.

Preheat oven to 350 degrees. For filling, arrange banana slices in single layer in crust. In a large bowl, whisk sugar, corn syrup, eggs, butter, vanilla, and rum flavoring until well blended. Whisk in melted chocolate.

Stir in pecans and ¹/₂ cup chocolate chips. Pour chocolate mixture over bananas. Bake 45 to 50 minutes or until top is dry and slightly cracked. Cool 15 minutes on a wire rack. Remove sides of pan and cool completely.

To decorate, place remaining ¹/₂ cup chocolate chips in a disposable pastry bag and microwave on medium power (50%) at 30 second intervals until melted. Cut tip of pastry bag to form a small hole and drizzle chocolate over top of tart. Allow chocolate to harden. Cut into squares to serve.

Yield: about 12 servings

116

CREAMY DESSERT CRÊPES

RASPBERRY CREAM FILLING
- 1 package (3 ounces) cream cheese, softened
- 1/4 cup seedless raspberry jam
- 1 tablespoon sour cream
- 1 tablespoon confectioners sugar
- 1/2 teaspoon vanilla extract

APRICOT-ORANGE CREAM FILLING
- 1 package (3 ounces) cream cheese, softened
- 1/2 cup sour cream
- 1/4 cup apricot preserves
- 1/4 teaspoon orange extract

CRÊPES
- 1 1/4 cups all-purpose flour
- 1 teaspoon sugar
- Pinch of salt
- 1 3/4 cups milk
- 2 eggs
- 1 1/2 tablespoons butter, melted

For raspberry cream filling, beat cream cheese in a small bowl until fluffy. Add jam, sour cream, confectioners sugar, and vanilla; beat until well blended. Cover and chill 2 hours.

For apricot-orange cream filling, beat cream cheese in a small bowl until fluffy. Add sour cream, preserves, and orange extract; beat until well blended. Cover and chill 2 hours.

For crêpes, combine flour, sugar, and salt in a medium bowl. Make a well in center of dry ingredients. Add remaining ingredients; beat until smooth. Cover and chill 1 hour.

Heat a lightly greased 8-inch skillet over medium heat. For each crêpe, spoon about 2 tablespoons batter into skillet. Tilt skillet to spread batter evenly in bottom of pan to form a 5 1/2-inch circle. Cook until lightly browned; turn and cook about 30 seconds. Place between layers of waxed paper. (Crêpes may be wrapped and stored in refrigerator.)

To serve, fold crêpes into quarters. Spoon about 1 tablespoon of desired cream filling into 1 section of each crêpe. Serve with Silky Chocolate Sauce.
Yield: about 2 dozen crêpes

For an elegant dessert, serve Creamy Dessert Crêpes with raspberry or apricot-orange fillings; finish with Silky Chocolate Sauce.

SILKY CHOCOLATE SAUCE

- 1 can (12 ounces) evaporated milk
- 1 package (6 ounces) semisweet chocolate chips
- 1/2 cup butter or margarine
- 2 cups confectioners sugar

In a heavy medium saucepan, combine evaporated milk, chocolate chips, and butter. Stirring constantly, cook over medium heat until smooth. Increase heat to medium-high. Gradually stir in confectioners sugar and bring to a boil. Stirring constantly, reduce heat to medium-low and boil 8 minutes. Remove from heat. Serve warm or at room temperature over Creamy Dessert Crêpes. Store in an airtight container in refrigerator.
Yield: about 2 1/2 cups sauce

CHOCOLATE CUSTARD

CUSTARD

    3 eggs, beaten
    1 package (6 ounces) semisweet
        chocolate chips
1 1/2 cups milk
  1/2 cup sugar
  1/4 teaspoon ground cinnamon

CHOCOLATE CURLS

    1 package (6 ounces) semisweet
        chocolate chips

DECORATIVE TOPPING

    2 tablespoons water
1 1/2 teaspoons unflavored gelatin
    2 tablespoons sugar
  1/2 cup whipping cream

Preheat oven to 325 degrees. For custard, place eggs in a small bowl. In a medium saucepan, melt chocolate chips over low heat. Stir in milk, sugar, and cinnamon. Increase heat to medium. Stirring constantly, bring to a simmer and cook until sugar dissolves. Add about 1/2 cup chocolate mixture to eggs; stir until well blended. Gradually add egg mixture to chocolate mixture in saucepan, stirring until well blended. Remove from heat. Place a greased 9-inch pie plate in a shallow roasting pan. Pour chocolate mixture into pie plate. Fill roasting pan with very hot water to come halfway up side of pie plate. Bake 55 to 60 minutes or until a knife inserted near center of custard comes out clean. Cool completely on a wire rack. Cover and refrigerate until well chilled.

For chocolate curls, melt chocolate chips in a small saucepan over low heat, stirring constantly. Pour onto an ungreased baking sheet, spreading chocolate to form a 3 x 6-inch rectangle. Refrigerate until set but not

A topping of sweetened whipped cream and chocolate curls crowns incredibly rich Chocolate Custard. Moist Peanut Butter-Cinnamon Brownies feature an unusual flavor combination.

firm. To make curls, pull a chocolate curler or vegetable peeler across surface of chocolate (curls will break if chocolate is too firm). Remelting and cooling chocolate as necessary, form desired number of curls. Refrigerate curls until ready to decorate.

For decorative topping, place a medium bowl and beaters from an electric mixer in freezer until well chilled. In a small saucepan, sprinkle gelatin over water; let stand 1 minute. Stir in sugar. Stirring constantly, cook over low heat about 5 minutes or until gelatin and sugar dissolve. Remove from heat. In chilled bowl, beat whipping cream until soft peaks form. Add sugar mixture and beat until stiff peaks form. Spoon topping into a pastry bag fitted with a large star tip; pipe decorations on custard. Garnish with chocolate curls. Store in an airtight container in refrigerator.
Yield: about 10 servings

PEANUT BUTTER-CINNAMON BROWNIES

  1/4 cup butter or margarine, melted
  1/2 cup granulated sugar
  1/2 cup firmly packed brown sugar
    2 eggs
    1 teaspoon vanilla extract
  1/2 cup all-purpose flour
    1 teaspoon ground cinnamon
  1/2 teaspoon baking powder
  1/2 teaspoon salt
  1/2 cup extra-crunchy peanut butter

Preheat oven to 350 degrees. In a medium bowl, combine butter and sugars. Add eggs and vanilla; beat until smooth. In a small bowl, combine flour, cinnamon, baking powder, and salt. Add dry ingredients to butter mixture; stir just until dry ingredients are moistened. Stir in peanut butter. Spread batter into a greased 7 x 11-inch metal baking pan. Bake 20 to 25 minutes or until set in center. Cool completely in pan. Cut into squares to serve.
Yield: about 2 dozen brownies

MAKING CHOCOLATE CURLS

Making chocolate curls for garnishes is not difficult, but it does take a little practice. The chocolate should be the correct firmness to form the curls, neither too soft nor too hard. Different types of baking chocolates may be used, but the most common ones are semisweet and unsweetened. They are packaged in boxes containing 1-ounce squares.

There are several methods for making chocolate curls. To make small, short curls, hold a baking chocolate square in your hand for a few minutes to slightly soften chocolate. Rub chocolate over shredding side (large holes) of a grater to form curls. For medium-size curls, use a vegetable peeler or chocolate curler (available in kitchen specialty shops) to shave the wide side (for wide curls) or thin side (for thin curls) of a chocolate square.

To make long, thin, loosely formed curls, melt 6 chocolate squares and pour into a foil-lined 3 1/4 x 5 1/4-inch loaf pan. Chill until chocolate is set (about 2 hours). Remove from pan and remove foil. Rub chocolate over shredding side (large holes) of a grater to form curls.

To make large curls, melt 5 chocolate squares and pour onto an ungreased baking sheet to form a 3 x 5-inch rectangle. Chill about 10 minutes. Scrape across surface of chocolate with a long metal spatula, knife, teaspoon, or chocolate curler to form curls. The spatula and knife will form long, thin curls and the teaspoon and curler will form shorter curls. Return pan to refrigerator if chocolate becomes too soft. Use a toothpick to pick up curls. Refrigerate curls until ready to decorate.

Easy-to-assemble Pear and Chocolate Trifle (clockwise from top left) introduces a delightful flavor combination. A hint of orange awakens creamy Chocolate Pâté, and a sprinkling of sugar tops our velvety Chocolate Cream Cake. The Chestnut Pound Cake is laced with brandy and chocolate chips.

CHESTNUT POUND CAKE

Look for canned chestnut spread at gourmet food stores.

2³/4 cups all-purpose flour
2 cups sugar
2 teaspoons baking soda
¹/2 teaspoon salt
3 eggs
¹/2 cup vegetable oil
1 can (17¹/2 ounces) chestnut spread
³/4 cup brandy, divided
1 teaspoon almond extract
1 package (12 ounces) semisweet chocolate chips

Preheat oven to 350 degrees. In a large bowl, combine flour, sugar, baking soda, and salt; stir until well blended. In a small bowl, combine eggs and oil; beat into flour mixture. Add chestnut spread, ¹/2 cup brandy, and almond extract; beat until well blended. Stir in chocolate chips. Pour batter into a greased and floured 9-inch springform pan. Bake about 1¹/4 hours or until toothpick inserted in center of cake comes out clean. Remove cake from oven and pour remaining ¹/4 cup brandy over warm cake. Cool cake in pan 1 hour. Remove sides of pan. Transfer to a serving plate.
Yield: 10 to 12 servings

CHOCOLATE PÂTÉ

16 ounces semisweet baking chocolate, chopped
1¹/4 cups butter, cut into pieces
8 eggs, separated
¹/2 cup orange-flavored liqueur
1 cup sugar
2¹/2 tablespoons water
¹/2 teaspoon cream of tartar
¹/4 teaspoon salt
Tubes of red and green decorating icing with a set of decorating tips

Stirring occasionally, melt chocolate and butter in top of a double boiler over hot water; pour into a medium bowl. In another medium bowl, beat egg yolks and liqueur until mixture lightens in color. Transfer egg mixture to top of a double boiler over simmering water. Stirring constantly, cook until mixture reaches 160 degrees on a thermometer (6 to 8 minutes). Fold yolk mixture into chocolate mixture; chill 45 minutes. Combine egg whites, sugar, water, cream of tartar, and salt in top of a double boiler. Whisking constantly, cook over simmering water until mixture reaches 160 degrees on a thermometer (about 25 minutes). Transfer mixture to a large bowl and beat until stiff peaks form. Fold into chocolate mixture. Pour into a 5 x 9-inch loaf pan lined with plastic wrap; cover and freeze until firm.

To serve, remove frozen pâté from pan. Use decorating icing to pipe holly onto pâté. Use a knife dipped in hot water to cut into thin slices. Serve immediately.
Yield: 10 to 12 servings

PEAR AND CHOCOLATE TRIFLE

24 ladyfingers
¹/2 cup seedless raspberry jam
1 can (29 ounces) pear halves, drained
2 packages (4 ounces each) milk chocolate instant pudding mix
2 cups half and half
¹/4 cup sugar
1 cup whipping cream
4 ounces semisweet baking chocolate, shaved

Split ladyfingers in half lengthwise and spread cut sides with jam. Line sides of a trifle or serving bowl with ladyfingers, placing every other one with jam-side facing side of bowl. Line bottom of bowl with ladyfingers, jam side up. Place pears on ladyfingers in bottom of bowl. Beat pudding mix with half and half until thickened. Pour into bowl. Gradually adding sugar, beat whipping cream until stiff peaks form. Spoon whipped cream mixture over top. Sprinkle with shaved chocolate. Cover loosely and refrigerate until ready to serve.
Yield: about 8 servings

CHOCOLATE CREAM CAKE

CAKE

¹/2 cup butter or margarine, softened
4 ounces cream cheese, softened
2 cups sugar
2 eggs, lightly beaten
2 teaspoons vanilla extract
2 cups all-purpose flour
³/4 cup cocoa
1¹/2 teaspoons baking soda
¹/2 teaspoon salt
1 cup boiling water

FROSTING

1 package (12 ounces) semisweet chocolate chips, melted and cooled to room temperature
1¹/2 cups sour cream
1 teaspoon vanilla extract
Confectioners sugar to decorate

Preheat oven to 350 degrees. For cake, cream butter, cream cheese, and sugar in a large bowl until fluffy. Beat in eggs and vanilla. In a small bowl, combine flour, cocoa, baking soda, and salt. Stir dry ingredients into creamed mixture. Stir in water. Pour batter into 2 greased and floured 9-inch round cake pans. Bake 25 to 30 minutes or until a toothpick inserted in center of cake comes out clean. Remove from pans and cool on a wire rack.

For frosting, beat melted chocolate, sour cream, and vanilla until smooth. Spread frosting between layers and on top and sides of cake. To decorate top, cut holly leaves and berries from white paper; arrange on top of cake. Sift confectioners sugar over top; carefully lift off paper pieces.
Yield: 10 to 12 servings

An Australian dessert named for a famous Russian ballerina, Pavlova with Strawberry-Orange Sauce is a sumptuous creation.

PAVLOVA WITH STRAWBERRY-ORANGE SAUCE

MERINGUE
- 4 egg whites
- 1 teaspoon vinegar
- 1 teaspoon vanilla extract
- 1/4 teaspoon cream of tartar
- 1/4 teaspoon salt
- 1 cup sugar

SAUCE
- 2 tablespoons cornstarch
- 1/4 cup orange juice
- 1 jar (12 ounces) strawberry preserves
- 1 package (10 ounces) frozen sweetened sliced strawberries, thawed
- 1/4 cup sugar plus 2 tablespoons sugar, divided
- 1 1/4 teaspoons grated orange zest
- 1/2 teaspoon salt
- 1 cup whipping cream

Preheat oven to 250 degrees. For meringue, draw a 9-inch-diameter circle on bottom side of parchment paper. Place paper on a baking sheet. In a medium bowl, beat egg whites, vinegar, vanilla, cream of tartar, and salt until soft peaks form. Gradually add sugar; beat until stiff peaks form. Spoon egg white mixture into circle. With back of spoon, make a slight hollow in center of mixture to hold whipped cream and sauce. Bake 1 1/2 hours. Carefully transfer parchment paper and warm meringue to a wire rack to cool completely (cracks may form).

For sauce, dissolve cornstarch in orange juice in a small bowl. In a medium saucepan over medium heat, combine strawberry preserves, strawberries, 1/4 cup sugar, orange zest, and salt. Cook 3 minutes or until preserves melt and sugar dissolves. Stir in cornstarch mixture. Stirring constantly, increase heat to medium high; cook 3 minutes or until mixture thickens. Remove from heat and chill 1 1/2 hours.

To serve, beat whipping cream in a medium bowl until soft peaks form. Add remaining 2 tablespoons sugar; beat until stiff peaks form. Spoon whipped cream onto meringue. Spoon sauce over whipped cream. Serve immediately.

Yield: about 8 servings

Mocha Pudding Cake is so rich and fudgy, guests will never believe it's low fat. Served warm with a dollop of light whipped topping, the dessert is a chocolate lover's heaven!

MOCHA PUDDING CAKE

1	cup all-purpose flour
3/4	cup granulated sugar
1/4	cup plus 2 tablespoons cocoa, divided
1 1/2	teaspoons baking powder
1/4	teaspoon salt
1/2	cup skim milk
2	tablespoons vegetable oil
1	teaspoon vanilla extract
1	cup firmly packed brown sugar
1 3/4	cups boiling strongly brewed coffee

9   tablespoons reduced-fat frozen whipped topping, thawed

Preheat oven to 350 degrees. Combine flour, granulated sugar, 2 tablespoons cocoa, baking powder, and salt in a 9-inch square baking pan. Add milk, oil, and vanilla; whisk until smooth. In a small bowl, combine brown sugar and remaining 1/4 cup cocoa; sprinkle over batter. Pour coffee over batter (do not stir).

Bake 40 to 45 minutes or until a toothpick inserted in cake portion comes out clean. Cool cake in pan 5 minutes. Top each serving with 1 tablespoon whipped topping.
Yield: 9 servings

1 serving: 270 calories, 4.1 grams fat, 2.8 grams protein, 55.2 grams carbohydrate

Low in fat but big on taste, Chocolate-Banana Cream Pie starts with a flaky crust, then layers of chocolate, banana slices, and vanilla pudding are covered with light, fluffy meringue.

CHOCOLATE-BANANA CREAM PIE

CRUST
- 3/4 cup sifted cake flour
- 1/2 teaspoon sugar
- 1/8 teaspoon salt
- 1/8 teaspoon baking powder
- 2 tablespoons chilled margarine, cut into pieces
- 2 tablespoons cold water
  Vegetable cooking spray

MERINGUE
- 3 egg whites
- 1/4 teaspoon cream of tartar
- 6 tablespoons sugar

FILLING
- 1 egg
- 1 egg yolk
- 1/2 cup sugar
- 3 tablespoons cornstarch
- 1/8 teaspoon salt
- 1 1/2 cups skim milk
- 1/2 teaspoon vanilla extract

- 1 ounce semisweet baking chocolate, chopped
- 1 banana, sliced

Preheat oven to 400 degrees. For crust, combine cake flour, sugar, salt, and baking powder in a medium bowl. Using a pastry blender or 2 knives, cut in margarine until mixture resembles coarse meal. Sprinkle with water; stir with a fork until moistened. Shape dough into a ball and place between 2 sheets of plastic wrap. Roll out dough into a 12-inch circle. Remove top sheet of plastic wrap. Invert dough into a 9-inch pie plate sprayed with cooking spray. Flute edges of dough. Prick bottom of crust with fork. Bake 12 minutes; cool completely.

Reduce oven temperature to 350 degrees. For meringue, beat egg whites at high speed of an electric mixer until foamy. Add cream of tartar; beat until soft peaks form. Add sugar, 1 tablespoon at a time, beating until sugar dissolves and stiff peaks form. Set meringue aside.

For filling, beat egg and egg yolk in a small bowl. Combine sugar, cornstarch, and salt in a heavy medium saucepan. Stir in milk. Stirring constantly, cook over medium heat about 11 minutes or until mixture thickens; remove from heat. Stir 1/4 cup milk mixture into beaten eggs. Stirring constantly, add egg mixture back into hot mixture in saucepan; cook 2 minutes. Remove from heat; stir in vanilla. Spoon 1/2 cup filling into a separate bowl; stir in chocolate until melted. Pour chocolate mixture into crust. Place banana slices over chocolate mixture. Pour remaining filling over slices. Spread meringue over hot filling, sealing edges to crust.

Filled with old-fashioned goodness, orange-flavored Swan Cake gets a holiday sparkle from decorative almond-shaped dragées.

Bake 15 to 20 minutes or until meringue is golden brown. Cool completely on a wire rack. Store in an airtight container in refrigerator.
Yield: 8 servings

1 serving: 223 calories, 4.1 grams fat, 5.4 grams protein, 42.5 grams carbohydrate

SWAN CAKE

Beating the dry ingredients with an electric mixer may be an unusual step, but it blends and aerates the ingredients, giving the cake its sponge-like texture.

CAKE
2¼ cups sifted cake flour
1¾ cups sugar
2 teaspoons baking powder
½ teaspoon salt
7 egg yolks
¾ cup orange juice

½ cup vegetable oil
2 teaspoons grated orange zest
2½ teaspoons orange extract
1 teaspoon vanilla extract
10 egg whites
1 teaspoon cream of tartar

FROSTING
1 cup butter, softened
1 package (8 ounces) cream cheese, softened
8 cups confectioners sugar
2 tablespoons milk
2 tablespoons orange juice
1 tablespoon orange extract
Silver almond-shaped dragées to decorate

Preheat oven to 325 degrees. For cake, combine flour, sugar, baking powder, and salt in a large bowl. Using an electric mixer, blend at low speed 1 minute. In a medium bowl, combine egg yolks, orange juice, oil, orange zest, and extracts; beat until well blended. Make a well in center of dry ingredients and add egg mixture; beat until smooth. In a medium bowl, combine egg whites and cream of tartar. Beat until soft peaks form. Carefully fold egg whites into batter. Pour batter into 3 greased 9-inch round cake pans lined with waxed paper. Bake 25 to 30 minutes or until a toothpick inserted in center of cake comes out clean. Cool in pans 10 minutes. Remove from pans and cool completely on a wire rack.

For frosting, cream butter and cream cheese until fluffy. Beat in confectioners sugar, milk, orange juice, and orange extract until smooth. Spread frosting between layers and on top and sides of cake. Decorate with dragées (remove dragées before serving).
Yield: 10 to 12 servings

until mixture is a deep golden brown. Remove from heat and immediately pour mixture into an 8-inch round cake pan, tilting to evenly coat bottom.

Preheat oven to 325 degrees. Combine milk and peanut butter in a medium saucepan. Whisking constantly, cook over medium heat until smooth and heated through; remove from heat. Combine egg substitute and remaining ¹/₂ cup sugar in a medium bowl; whisk until well blended. Gradually add milk mixture to egg mixture, stirring well. Pour mixture over caramelized sugar in cake pan. Place in a 9 x 13-inch baking pan. Add hot water to baking pan to come halfway up sides of cake pan. Bake 1 hour or until a knife inserted in center comes out clean. Transfer cake pan to a wire rack to cool. Cover and chill overnight. Unmold onto a serving plate.

Yield: 12 servings

1 serving: 147 calories, 2.9 grams fat, 5.5 grams protein, 25.6 grams carbohydrate

PEPPERMINT CHEESECAKE SQUARES

CRUST
²/₃ cup graham cracker crumbs
1¹/₂ tablespoons sugar
1 tablespoon reduced-calorie margarine, softened
Vegetable cooking spray

CHEESECAKE
12 ounces Neufchâtel cheese, softened
1 cup nonfat cottage cheese
¹/₂ cup sugar
2 tablespoons white crème de menthe
1 teaspoon vanilla extract
³/₄ cup nonfat egg substitute
¹/₂ cup crushed peppermint candies

Preheat oven to 350 degrees. For crust, combine cracker crumbs, sugar, and margarine in a small bowl. Press crumb mixture evenly into bottom of a 7 x11-inch baking dish sprayed with

Custard-like Peanut Butter Crème Caramel (top) is a gourmet delight with a healthier twist. Flavorful and creamy, our reduced-fat Peppermint Cheesecake Squares are laced with white crème de menthe.

PEANUT BUTTER CRÈME CARAMEL

1¹/₄ cups sugar, divided
¹/₄ cup water
¹/₄ teaspoon cream of tartar
2¹/₄ cups 2% milk
¹/₄ cup reduced-calorie smooth peanut butter
1¹/₄ cups nonfat egg substitute

In a small saucepan, combine ³/₄ cup sugar, water, and cream of tartar. Stirring constantly, cook over medium-low heat until sugar dissolves. Increase heat to medium and bring mixture to a boil. Without stirring, cook 10 to 15 minutes or

cooking spray. Bake 5 minutes. Cool on a wire rack.

For cheesecake, process Neufchâtel cheese, cottage cheese, sugar, crème de menthe, and vanilla in a food processor until smooth. Add egg substitute; process just until blended. Pour batter over crust. Bake 25 to 28 minutes or until mixture is almost set. Cool 45 minutes on a wire rack. Cover and chill 6 hours.

To serve, sprinkle crushed candies over cheesecake. Cut into 2-inch squares. Serve immediately.

Yield: 15 servings

1 serving: 169 calories, 6.8 grams fat, 5.5 grams protein, 20.1 grams carbohydrate

COCONUT CHRISTMAS PIE

CRUST
1½ cups all-purpose flour
½ teaspoon salt
½ cup vegetable shortening
3 to 4 tablespoons cold water

FILLING
1 cup sugar, divided
¼ cup all-purpose flour
1 envelope unflavored gelatin
½ teaspoon salt
1 can (8½ ounces) cream of coconut
1 cup milk
1 cup grated sweetened frozen coconut, divided
1 tablespoon clear vanilla extract
3 egg whites
1 tablespoon water
¼ teaspoon cream of tartar
½ cup whipping cream, whipped

Preheat oven to 450 degrees. For crust, combine flour and salt in a small bowl. Using a pastry blender or 2 knives, cut in shortening until mixture resembles coarse meal. Sprinkle with water; mix until a soft dough forms. On a lightly floured surface, use a floured rolling pin to roll out dough to ⅛-inch thickness. Transfer to a 9-inch pie plate and use a sharp knife to trim edge of

Loaded with sweetened coconut, a yummy filling tops a flaky homemade crust to make our Coconut Christmas Pie.

dough. Flute edge of crust. Prick bottom of crust with a fork. Bake 10 to 12 minutes or until lightly browned. Cool on a wire rack.

For filling, combine ½ cup sugar, flour, gelatin, and salt in a heavy medium saucepan; stir until well blended. Whisk in cream of coconut and milk. Whisking constantly, cook over medium heat until mixture boils; boil 2 minutes. Transfer mixture to a heatproof medium bowl. Set bowl in a larger bowl containing ice water. Stirring mixture frequently, let cool 15 minutes.

Stir ½ cup coconut and vanilla into filling. Place egg whites, remaining ½ cup sugar, water, and cream of tartar in the top of a double boiler over simmering water. Whisking constantly, cook until egg whites reach 160 degrees on a thermometer (about 10 minutes). Transfer egg whites to a large bowl; beat until soft peaks form. Fold beaten egg whites and whipped cream into filling. Spoon filling into pie shell. Sprinkle remaining ½ cup coconut over pie filling. Cover and chill 2 hours or until pie is firm.

Yield: about 8 servings

CARAMEL-PECAN CHEESECAKE

CRUST
- 2 cups butter-pecan cookie crumbs (about 15 cookies)
- 2 tablespoons butter or margarine, melted
- 2 tablespoons sugar

FILLING
- 3 packages (8 ounces each) cream cheese, softened
- 1 cup firmly packed brown sugar
- 2 tablespoons all-purpose flour
- 4 eggs
- 1/2 cup sour cream
- 1 teaspoon vanilla-butter-nut flavoring
- 1/4 teaspoon salt

TOPPING
- 1/2 cup sweetened condensed milk
- 1/3 cup light corn syrup
- 1/4 cup granulated sugar
- 3 tablespoons firmly packed brown sugar
- 3 tablespoons butter or margarine
- 1 tablespoon whipping cream
- 1/2 teaspoon vanilla-butter-nut flavoring
- 1/3 cup finely chopped toasted pecans

For crust, combine cookie crumbs, melted butter, and sugar in a small bowl. Press crumb mixture into bottom of an ungreased 9-inch springform pan. Cover and chill 30 minutes.

Preheat oven to 325 degrees. For filling, beat cream cheese in a large bowl until fluffy. Add brown sugar and flour; beat until well blended. Add eggs, 1 at a time, beating well after each addition. Add sour cream, vanilla-butter-nut flavoring, and salt; beat until well blended. Pour filling into chilled crust. Bake 55 to 65 minutes or until center is almost set. Turn oven off. Leave cake in oven 1 hour with door partially open. Remove cake from oven and cool completely in pan on a wire rack. Cover and chill 4 hours.

For topping, combine sweetened condensed milk, corn syrup, and sugars in a heavy medium saucepan over medium heat. Attach a candy thermometer to pan, making sure thermometer does not touch bottom of pan. Stirring constantly, cook until syrup reaches 220 degrees. Remove from heat. Stir in butter, whipping cream, and vanilla-butter-nut flavoring. Cool topping 30 minutes.

To serve, remove sides of pan. Press pecans onto side of cheesecake. Slowly pour caramel topping to within 1/2-inch of edges (topping will flow). Cut cheesecake with a wet knife, cleaning after each cut. Serve any remaining topping with cheesecake.

Yield: about 16 servings

COCONUT POUND CAKE

CAKE
- 1 1/2 cups butter or margarine, softened
- 3 cups sugar
- 6 eggs
- 3 cups all-purpose flour
- 1/4 teaspoon baking soda
- 1 container (8 ounces) sour cream
- 1 teaspoon coconut extract
- 1 teaspoon rum extract
- 1 cup flaked coconut

SYRUP
- 1 cup water
- 1 cup sugar
- 1 teaspoon almond extract

Preheat oven to 325 degrees. For cake, cream butter and sugar in a large bowl. Add eggs, 1 at a time, beating well after each addition. Sift flour and baking soda into a medium bowl. Alternately beat dry ingredients, sour cream, and extracts into creamed mixture. Stir in coconut. Spoon batter into a greased 10-inch fluted tube pan. Bake 1 1/4 to 1 1/2 hours or until a toothpick inserted in center of cake comes out clean. Cool cake in pan 15 minutes.

For syrup, combine water and sugar in a medium saucepan. Stirring frequently, cook over medium-high heat 5 minutes. Remove from heat and stir in almond extract. Before removing cake from pan, brush about one-third of warm syrup on cake. Invert cake onto a serving plate. Brush remaining syrup on cake. Allow cake to cool completely. Store in an airtight container.

Yield: about 16 servings

Caramel-Pecan Cheesecake (left) *has a nutty cookie crumb crust, a rich filling, and a caramel topping that's oh-so-good! Coconut Pound Cake is a moist tropical creation.*

OATMEAL-WALNUT SCONES

1 cup all-purpose flour
2/3 cup whole-wheat flour
1/3 cup sugar
1 1/2 teaspoons baking powder
3/4 teaspoon baking soda
1/4 teaspoon salt
3/4 cup chilled butter or margarine, cut into pieces
1 1/4 cups quick-cooking oats
3/4 cup finely chopped walnuts, toasted
3/4 cup buttermilk
1/2 teaspoon vanilla extract
1 egg, lightly beaten

Preheat oven to 350 degrees. Combine flours, sugar, baking powder, baking soda, and salt in a large bowl. Using a pastry blender or 2 knives, cut in butter until mixture resembles fine meal. Stir in oats and walnuts. Add buttermilk and vanilla; stir just until mixture is blended. On a lightly floured surface, pat dough to 1/2-inch thickness. Use a 3-inch-diameter round cookie cutter dipped in flour to cut out scones. Place 1 inch apart on a lightly greased baking sheet. Brush tops of scones with beaten egg. Bake 18 to 22 minutes or until scones are lightly browned. Serve warm.
Yield: about 15 scones

MAPLE-PECAN COOKIES

3/4 cup butter or margarine, softened
1 cup firmly packed brown sugar
1 egg
1/4 cup maple syrup
1 teaspoon vanilla extract
1/4 teaspoon orange extract
1 cup all-purpose flour
1/2 teaspoon baking powder
1 1/4 cups chopped pecans, toasted and finely chopped
1/2 cup quick-cooking oats

Preheat oven to 375 degrees. In a large bowl, cream butter and brown sugar until fluffy. Add egg, maple syrup, and extracts; beat until well blended. In a small bowl, combine flour and baking powder. Add dry ingredients to creamed mixture; stir until a soft dough forms. Stir in pecans and oats. Drop teaspoonfuls of dough 2 inches apart on an ungreased baking sheet. Bake 7 to 9 minutes or until edges are lightly browned. Cool cookies on baking sheet 2 minutes; transfer to a wire rack to cool completely. Store in an airtight container.
Yield: about 5 dozen cookies

CHOCOLATE-ALMOND BISCOTTI

1/2 cup butter or margarine, softened
1/2 cup firmly packed brown sugar
1/2 cup granulated sugar
3 eggs
1 teaspoon almond extract
2 1/2 cups all-purpose flour
1 teaspoon baking powder
1/2 teaspoon baking soda
1/8 teaspoon salt
1 cup semisweet chocolate mini chips
1 cup coarsely ground almonds, toasted

Preheat oven to 375 degrees. In a large bowl, cream butter and sugars until fluffy. Add eggs and almond extract; beat until smooth. In a medium bowl, combine flour, baking powder, baking soda, and salt. Add dry ingredients to creamed mixture; stir until a soft dough forms. Stir in chocolate chips and almonds. Divide dough in half. On a greased and floured baking sheet, shape each piece of dough into a 2 1/2 x 10-inch loaf, flouring hands as necessary. Allow 3 inches between loaves on baking sheet. Bake 20 to 24 minutes or until loaves are firm and lightly browned; cool 10 minutes on baking sheet.

Cut loaves diagonally into 1/2-inch slices. Lay slices flat on an ungreased baking sheet. Bake 5 to 7 minutes; turn slices over and bake 5 to 7 minutes longer or until golden brown. Transfer cookies to a wire rack to cool. Store in a cookie tin.
Yield: about 3 dozen cookies

You'll love this sampling of coffee-shop favorites, which includes hearty Oatmeal-Walnut Scones (clockwise from top left), chewy Maple-Pecan Cookies, and a favorite for dunking in coffee or cocoa — Chocolate-Almond Biscotti.

GIFTS OF GOOD TASTE

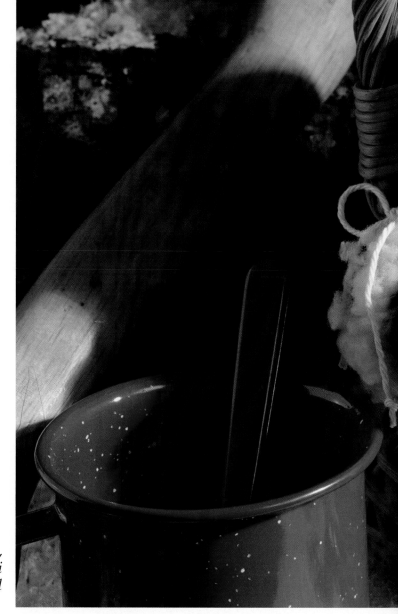

What makes a gift special is the thought and care that go into choosing it, and — in the case of these treats from the kitchen — creating it! A gift of food says, "I know what you like; let me pamper you." This assortment of recipes has something to delight the taste buds of everyone on your gift list, whether they prefer delicious candies, jams, and breads or mouth-watering muffins, sauces, and snack mixes. You'll even find wholesome, homemade doggie biscuits for Fido!

For a hearty heat-and-eat dinner, make up a batch of spicy White Chili (recipe on page 134). It'll ease the chill of a winter day.

WHITE CHILI (Shown on page 133)

- 2 tablespoons vegetable oil
- 1 medium white onion, finely chopped
- 1 can (4$\frac{1}{2}$ ounces) chopped green chiles
- 2 teaspoons garlic powder
- 2 teaspoons salt
- 2 teaspoons ground cumin
- 2 teaspoons ground oregano
- 2 teaspoons ground coriander
- $\frac{1}{2}$ teaspoon cayenne pepper
- 2 cans (15.8 ounces each) great Northern beans
- 2 cans (10$\frac{1}{2}$ ounces each) chicken broth
- 2 cans (5 ounces each) chicken, drained

In a large stockpot, heat oil over medium heat. Add onion; sauté until tender. Add green chiles, garlic powder, salt, cumin, oregano, coriander, and cayenne pepper; stir until well blended. Stir in undrained beans, chicken broth, and chicken. Bring to a boil; reduce heat to low and simmer 15 to 20 minutes or until heated through. Serve warm. Store in an airtight container in refrigerator.
Yield: 8 to 10 servings

COOKIE PIZZAS

- Vegetable cooking spray
- 1 package (18 ounces) refrigerated peanut butter cookie dough
- 1 jar (10 ounces) maraschino cherries, drained and halved
- 1 cup peanuts
- 1 package (6 ounces) semisweet chocolate chips
- 8 ounces vanilla candy coating, melted

Use the bottom of an 8-inch round cake pan as a pattern to draw 4 circles on cardboard; cut out and set aside. Preheat oven to 350 degrees. Spray 8-inch round cake pan with vegetable spray until well coated. Divide cookie dough into fourths. With floured hands, press one

Use your imagination to top tasty Cookie Pizzas with a variety of nuts, candies, and icing. The giant treats will please teachers, friends, and co-workers.

fourth of dough into cake pan. Bake 8 to 10 minutes. Carefully remove from pan and cool on a wire rack. Repeat with remaining cookie dough.

Place cookies on cardboard circles. Place cherries, peanuts, and chocolate chips on cookies. Drizzle candy coating over cookies; let harden. Store in an airtight container.
Yield: 4 cookie pizzas, 6 servings each

134

Easy-to-make Mocha Sugar adds rich flavor to coffee, espresso, or cappuccino. It's just the thing for a coffee lover.

MOCHA SUGAR

1¹/₄ cups sugar
3 tablespoons coffee-flavored liqueur
¹/₂ teaspoon ground cinnamon

In a small bowl, stir sugar, liqueur, and cinnamon until well blended. Store in an airtight container. Give with serving suggestion.

Yield: about 1 cup flavored sugar

To serve: Stir desired amount of sugar into coffee.

Send wishes for a Merry "Crisp-mas" with Cinnamon Crunch candy! It's not hard to make — simply top store-bought grahams with walnuts and a praline mixture, bake, and enjoy.

CINNAMON CRUNCH

12 cinnamon graham crackers
   (2¹/₂ x 5 inches each)
2 cups finely chopped walnuts
1 cup butter
1 cup firmly packed brown sugar
¹/₂ teaspoon ground cinnamon

Preheat oven to 400 degrees. Arrange cinnamon graham crackers in a single layer with sides touching in bottom of a greased 10¹/₂ x 15¹/₂-inch jellyroll pan. Sprinkle walnuts evenly over crackers.

In a heavy small saucepan, combine butter, brown sugar, and cinnamon. Stirring constantly, cook over medium heat until sugar dissolves and mixture begins to boil. Continue to boil syrup 3 minutes longer without stirring; pour over crackers. Bake 8 to 10 minutes or until bubbly and slightly darker around the edges. Cool completely in pan. Break into pieces. Store in an airtight container.

Yield: about 1¹/₂ pounds candy

BRANDIED FRUITCAKE

1 cup chopped dried apricots
1 cup golden raisins
¹/₄ cup orange-flavored liqueur
2 cups butter, softened
2 cups sugar
6 eggs
¹/₂ cup brandy
1 teaspoon vanilla extract
4 cups all-purpose flour, divided
2 teaspoons baking powder
1 teaspoon ground cinnamon
1 teaspoon ground allspice
¹/₂ teaspoon salt
3 cups chopped pecans
1 cup chopped candied orange
   peel
1 cup chopped candied pineapple
1 cup candied red cherry halves
1 cup candied green cherry halves
3 tablespoons light corn syrup
1 tablespoon hot water
   Pecan halves and candied red
      and green cherry halves to
      decorate
   Brandy

Chock-full of candied fruits and chopped nuts, a miniature Brandied Fruitcake is a spirited Yuletide offering.

In a medium bowl, combine apricots, raisins, and liqueur. Allow to stand 2 hours, stirring occasionally.

Preheat oven to 325 degrees. Line four 4¹/₂ x 8¹/₂-inch loaf pans with waxed paper; grease waxed paper. In a very large bowl, cream butter and sugar until fluffy. Add eggs; beat until smooth. Stir in brandy and vanilla. In a medium bowl, combine 3 cups flour, baking powder, cinnamon, allspice, and salt. Add dry ingredients to creamed mixture; beat until well blended.

In a large bowl, combine pecans, orange peel, pineapple, and cherry halves. Stir in remaining 1 cup flour; stir until fruit is coated. Add both fruit mixtures to cake batter; stir until well blended. Spoon batter into prepared pans. Bake 40 minutes. Remove from oven. Combine corn syrup and hot water in a small bowl. Brush corn syrup mixture over top of each loaf. Decorate each loaf with pecans and candied cherry halves. Brush again with corn syrup mixture. Bake 5 minutes longer or until a toothpick inserted in center of cake comes out clean. If cake begins to brown too much, loosely cover with aluminum foil. Cool in pans 15 minutes. Remove from pans and cool completely on a wire rack. Wrap each loaf in a large piece of brandy-soaked cheesecloth, then in heavy-duty aluminum foil. Loaves can be served at this time or drizzled with 2 tablespoons brandy once a week for 4 weeks. Store in a cool place.

Yield: 4 fruitcakes

A flaky pastry crust and a creamy plum filling make tiny Sugarplum Tarts extra special. The little pies are sure to become a holiday tradition.

SUGARPLUM TARTS

CRUST

- 3/4 cup butter or margarine, softened
- 1/2 cup sugar
- 2 egg yolks
- 1 3/4 cups all-purpose flour
- 1/8 teaspoon salt
- 3/4 teaspoon vanilla extract

FILLING

- 1 jar (10 ounces) red plum jam
- 1 cup sugar
- 1/4 cup all-purpose flour
- 1/8 teaspoon salt
- 1 cup whipping cream
- 1/2 cup half and half
- 2 teaspoons vanilla extract

Preheat oven to 350 degrees. For crust, cream butter and sugar in a large bowl until fluffy. Add egg yolks, 1 at a time, beating well after each addition. Add remaining ingredients; stir until a soft dough forms. Press about 1 1/2 teaspoons dough into bottoms and up sides of greased miniature muffin tins.

For filling, spoon about 1/2 teaspoon jam into bottom of each crust; set aside. Sift next 3 ingredients into a large bowl. Add remaining ingredients. Using highest speed of an electric mixer, beat cream mixture until thick and fluffy, about 4 to 5 minutes. Spoon about 1 tablespoon cream mixture into each crust. Bake 30 to 35 minutes or until filling is set in center and crust is brown. Cool in pan 10 minutes. Transfer to a wire rack to cool completely.

Yield: about 5 dozen tarts

Mint Tea Mix mingles the citrusy bouquet of orange peel and the spicy flavor of cloves with mint leaves for a refreshing blend.

MINT TEA MIX

- 1 1/2 cups loose tea leaves
- 1 jar (0.25 ounce) dried mint leaves
- 2 tablespoons dried orange peel
- 2 tablespoons whole cloves

Combine tea leaves, mint leaves, orange peel, and cloves in a medium bowl; stir until well blended. Store in an airtight container. Give with serving instructions.

Yield: about 1 3/4 cups tea mix

To serve: For 1 cup of tea, place 1 teaspoon tea mix in an individual tea infuser. Pour 1 cup boiling water over tea mix. Allow tea to steep 3 to 5 minutes. Remove infuser; serve hot.

For 1 quart of tea, place 2 tablespoons tea mix in a teapot. Pour 1 quart boiling water over tea mix. Allow tea to steep 3 to 5 minutes. Strain tea; serve hot.

APPLE-CINNAMON COOKIES

COOKIES

1 cup butter or margarine,
 softened
1½ cups firmly packed brown
 sugar
2 eggs
⅓ cup apple jelly
1 teaspoon vanilla extract
4 cups all-purpose flour
1 teaspoon ground cinnamon
½ teaspoon salt

ICING

3 cups confectioners sugar
3 tablespoons plus 1 teaspoon
 milk
 Brown and red paste food
 coloring

For cookies, cream butter and brown sugar in a large bowl until fluffy. Add eggs, apple jelly, and vanilla; stir until smooth. Sift flour, cinnamon, and salt into another large bowl. Add dry ingredients to creamed mixture; stir until a soft dough forms. Cover and chill 30 minutes.

Preheat oven to 350 degrees. On a lightly floured surface, use a floured rolling pin to roll out dough to ¼-inch thickness. Use a 2¾ x 3-inch apple-shaped cookie cutter to cut out cookies. Transfer to a greased baking sheet. Use a drinking straw to make a hole in stem of each cookie. Bake 14 to 16 minutes or until edges are lightly browned. Transfer to a wire rack to cool completely.

For icing, combine confectioners sugar and milk in a medium bowl; stir until smooth. Transfer ¼ cup icing to a small bowl; tint brown. Tint remaining icing red. Ice apples with red icing and stems with brown icing. Allow icing to harden. Store in an airtight container until ready to decorate tree.
Yield: about 4 dozen cookies

Delight a favorite teacher with a tabletop tree decorated with Apple-Cinnamon Cookies and an old-fashioned popcorn garland.

Here's a saucy gift idea — a jar of Creamy Tarragon or Sweet and Sour Sauce. Both are perfect for dipping seafood, poultry, or beef, or they can be served on the side with an entrée.

CREAMY TARRAGON SAUCE

- 1/4 cup butter or margarine
- 1 tablespoon all-purpose flour
- 1 cup milk
- 1/2 cup sour cream
- 1 teaspoon dried tarragon leaves
- 1 teaspoon dried chervil leaves
- 1 teaspoon dried basil leaves
- 1 teaspoon garlic powder
- 1/2 teaspoon salt
- 1/2 teaspoon ground black pepper

Melt butter in a medium saucepan over medium heat; stir in flour. Cook 1 to 2 minutes or until flour is browned. Gradually add milk, whisking constantly until sauce is smooth and thickens; remove from heat. Whisk in sour cream, tarragon, chervil, basil, garlic powder, salt, and pepper. Store in an airtight container in refrigerator. Give with serving instructions.

Yield: about 1 1/2 cups sauce

To serve: Transfer sauce to a medium saucepan. Cook over medium heat 3 to 5 minutes or until heated through, stirring occasionally. Serve warm with meat.

SWEET AND SOUR SAUCE

- 2 cups dry sherry
- 6 tablespoons honey
- 6 tablespoons red wine vinegar
- 2 tablespoons soy sauce
- 8 cloves garlic, minced
- 1/2 teaspoon salt
- 2 tablespoons cornstarch
- 1/4 cup water

Boil sherry in a medium saucepan over medium heat 10 to 12 minutes. Whisk in honey, vinegar, soy sauce, garlic, and salt; remove from heat. In a small bowl, combine cornstarch and water to make a paste. Return sauce to heat; whisk in cornstarch mixture. Cook 3 to 5 minutes or until sauce thickens. Store in an airtight container. Give with serving instructions.

Yield: about 1 1/2 cups sauce

To serve: Transfer sauce to a medium saucepan. Cook over medium heat 3 to 5 minutes or until heated through, stirring occasionally. Serve warm with meat.

Loaves of moist, nutty Cinnamon-Carrot Bread have down-home appeal! The yummy streusel topping is a snap to make using graham cracker crumbs. An old-fashioned favorite with a holiday twist, cinnamon-spiced Candied Apple Butter is delicious with biscuits or muffins.

CANDIED APPLE BUTTER

6 cups applesauce
3 cups firmly packed brown sugar
1/2 cup small red cinnamon
    candies
1 teaspoon ground cinnamon
1/4 teaspoon ground allspice

Combine applesauce, brown sugar, candies, cinnamon, and allspice in a heavy Dutch oven. Stirring constantly, cook over medium heat until candies melt and sugar dissolves. Reduce heat to medium low. Stirring occasionally,

simmer uncovered about 40 minutes or until mixture thickens. Cool and store in an airtight container in refrigerator.

Yield: about 6 1/2 cups apple butter

CINNAMON-CARROT BREAD

BREAD

- 3/4 cup coarsely crushed cinnamon graham crackers (about five 2 1/2 x 5-inch crackers)
- 3/4 cup chopped pecans
- 1 cup sugar
- 3/4 cup vegetable oil
- 2 eggs
- 1/2 teaspoon orange extract
- 1 cup shredded carrots
- 1 1/3 cups all-purpose flour
- 1 teaspoon ground cinnamon
- 1/2 teaspoon salt
- 1/2 teaspoon baking powder

ICING

- 3/4 cup confectioners sugar
- 1 tablespoon water
- 1/2 teaspoon orange extract

Preheat oven to 350 degrees. For bread, grease four 2 1/2 x 5-inch loaf pans. Line pans with waxed paper; grease waxed paper. In a medium bowl, combine cracker crumbs and pecans; set aside. In a large bowl, combine sugar, oil, eggs, and orange extract; beat until blended. Stir in carrots. In a small bowl, combine flour, cinnamon, salt, and baking powder. Add flour mixture to oil mixture; stir just until moistened. Spoon half of batter into prepared pans. Sprinkle about 3 tablespoons crumb mixture over batter in each pan; swirl mixture with a knife. Spoon remaining batter over crumb mixture. Sprinkle remaining crumb mixture on top. Bake 38 to 43 minutes or until a toothpick inserted in center of bread comes out clean and top is golden brown. Cool in pans 10 minutes. Remove from pans and cool completely on a wire rack.

For icing, combine confectioners sugar, water, and orange extract in a small bowl; stir until smooth. Drizzle icing over bread. Allow icing to harden. Store in an airtight container.

Yield: 4 loaves bread

Get the kids involved in making tasty gifts for their friends! They'll love these whimsical snack mixes — Please Don't Feed the Animals (with animal crackers), Something for the Elephants (with peanuts, of course!), and Go Fishin' (with gummy fish).

SOMETHING FOR THE ELEPHANTS

- 2 cups candy corn
- 2 cups candy-coated chocolate pieces
- 2 cups unsalted peanuts

Combine candy corn, chocolate pieces, and peanuts in a large bowl. Store in an airtight container.

Yield: 6 cups snack mix

GO FISHIN'

- 2 cups gummy fish
- 2 cups yogurt-covered peanuts
- 2 cups small pretzels

Combine gummy fish, peanuts, and pretzels in a large bowl. Store in an airtight container.

Yield: 6 cups snack mix

PLEASE DON'T FEED THE ANIMALS

- 2 cups animal crackers
- 2 cups chocolate- or carob-covered raisins
- 1 cup jelly beans
- 1 cup unsalted peanuts

Combine crackers, raisins, jelly beans, and peanuts in a large bowl. Store in an airtight container.

Yield: 6 cups snack mix

Enriched with oats and honey and "dressed" in a scarf and cap, a loaf of Snowman Bread will make a tasty treat on a busy morning.

SNOWMAN BREAD

- 2 cups water
- 1 cup old-fashioned rolled oats
- 6 cups all-purpose flour
- 1/2 cup nonfat dry milk powder
- 2 1/2 teaspoons salt
- 2 packages dry yeast
- 1/3 cup warm water
- 1/2 cup honey
- 1/4 cup vegetable oil
  Vegetable cooking spray
- 1 egg, beaten
  Raisins
  Candied cherry
  Pretzels

In a medium saucepan, bring 2 cups water to a boil. Remove from heat; stir in oats. Cool to room temperature.

Sift next 3 ingredients into a large bowl. In a small bowl, dissolve yeast in 1/3 cup warm water. Add oat mixture, yeast mixture, honey, and oil to dry ingredients. Stir until a soft dough forms. Turn onto a lightly floured surface and knead until dough becomes smooth and elastic. Place in a large bowl sprayed with cooking spray, turning once to coat top of dough. Cover and let rise in a warm place (80 to 85 degrees) 1 hour or until doubled in size.

Turn dough onto a lightly floured surface and punch down. Divide dough in half. Referring to photo, shape each half of dough into 3 balls, graduated in size. Arrange each set of balls on a greased baking sheet to resemble a snowman. Brush dough with egg. For each snowman, use raisins for eyes, mouth, and buttons and a small piece of candied cherry for nose. Break pretzels into twig shapes. Insert 1 broken pretzel into each side of snowmen for arms. Spray dough with cooking spray, cover, and let rise in a warm place 1 hour or until doubled in size.

Preheat oven to 350 degrees. Bake 25 to 30 minutes or until bread sounds hollow when tapped. Transfer to a wire rack to cool. Store in an airtight container.

Yield: 2 loaves bread

Don't forget your four-legged friends at Christmastime! These beef-flavored Dog Bones are prepared with wholesome ingredients.

DOG BONES

- 2 1/4 cups whole-wheat flour
- 1/2 cup nonfat dry milk powder
- 1 egg
- 1/2 cup vegetable oil
- 1 beef bouillon cube dissolved in 1/2 cup hot water
- 1 tablespoon firmly packed brown sugar

Preheat oven to 300 degrees. In a large bowl, combine all ingredients, stirring until well blended. Knead dough 2 minutes. On a floured surface, use a floured rolling pin to roll out dough to 1/4-inch thickness. Use a 2 1/2-inch-long bone-shaped cookie cutter to cut out bones. Bake 30 minutes on an ungreased baking sheet. Remove from pan and cool on wire rack. Store in an airtight container.

Yield: about 4 dozen dog bones

With our Chocolate-Mint Cheese Ball Mix, a friend can make a sweet, creamy dessert spread in no time. Be sure to include the instructions and add some cookies for munching.

CHOCOLATE-MINT CHEESE BALL MIX

1 package (12 ounces)
    semisweet chocolate chips
2 cups chopped pecans, toasted
1 cup 1-inch round peppermint
    candies (about 36 candies
    or 7 ounces)
    Cookies to serve

Process chocolate chips, pecans, and candies in a large food processor until finely ground. Place about 1½ cups mix in each of 4 resealable plastic bags. Give with cookies and recipe for making cheese ball.
Yield: about 6 cups mix, enough to make 4 cheese balls

To make cheese ball: Use an electric mixer to combine 1½ cups mix and one 8-ounce package softened cream cheese. Shape into a ball; wrap in plastic wrap and refrigerate until firm.

To serve, let stand at room temperature 20 to 30 minutes or until softened. Serve with cookies.
Yield: 1 cheese ball

CRANBERRY-RASPBERRY FREEZER JAM

1 cup fresh cranberries
1 package (12 ounces) frozen
    whole red raspberries, thawed
4 cups sugar
1 pouch (3 ounces) liquid fruit
    pectin
2 tablespoons lemon juice

Process cranberries in a food processor until coarsely chopped. Add raspberries; process until finely chopped. Combine fruit and sugar in a large bowl. Allow fruit mixture to stand 10 minutes, stirring occasionally. In a small bowl, combine liquid fruit pectin and lemon juice. Add pectin mixture to fruit mixture; stir constantly 3 minutes or until most of sugar dissolves. Spoon jam into jars; cover and allow jam to stand at room temperature 24 hours. Store in freezer. Place in

Fresh cranberries add a seasonal twist to tart, tangy Cranberry-Raspberry Freezer Jam. You'll want to share with all your friends!

refrigerator 1 hour before serving. May be refrozen. Keeps up to 3 weeks in refrigerator or up to 1 year in freezer.
Yield: about 5 cups jam

A basket of piping hot Orange-Pumpkin Muffins makes a sweet offering for anyone on your gift list.

ORANGE-PUMPKIN MUFFINS

1 3/4 cups all-purpose flour
1 1/2 teaspoons pumpkin pie spice
1 teaspoon baking soda
1/2 teaspoon baking powder
1/2 teaspoon salt
1 cup granulated sugar
1/2 cup firmly packed brown sugar
2 eggs
1/3 cup vegetable oil
1 cup canned pumpkin
1/3 cup orange juice
1 teaspoon grated orange zest
1/2 cup chopped walnuts

Preheat oven to 350 degrees. In a small bowl, combine flour, pumpkin pie spice, baking soda, baking powder, and salt. In a large bowl, combine sugars, eggs, and oil. Add pumpkin, orange juice, and orange zest to sugar mixture; beat until well blended. Stir in dry ingredients just until blended. Fill paper-lined muffin cups about two-thirds full. Sprinkle about 1 teaspoon walnuts over batter in each cup. Bake 20 to 23 minutes or until a toothpick inserted in center of muffin comes out clean. Transfer muffins to a wire rack to cool. Store in an airtight container.
Yield: about 1 1/2 dozen muffins

PEPPER SAUCE

5 medium green and red hot peppers, washed, stemmed, and chopped
3 cups white vinegar

Place peppers in a 1-quart glass jar with a nonmetal lid. Bring vinegar to a simmer over medium heat. Pour vinegar over peppers and allow to cool. Cover and let stand at room temperature 1 week to let flavors blend.

Strain vinegar into gift bottles. Store in refrigerator up to 1 month.
Yield: 3 cups sauce

This zesty duo is a great gourmet gift. The Pepper Sauce adds snap to vegetables and other foods, and the Raspberry Vinegar adds zing to salads or favorite recipes.

RASPBERRY VINEGAR

2 packages (12 ounces each) frozen raspberries
3 cups red rice wine vinegar

Crush raspberries and combine with vinegar in a large non-aluminum saucepan; add vinegar. Bring to a boil over medium-high heat; boil 3 minutes. Transfer mixture to a heatproof nonmetal container. Cover and let stand at room temperature 1 week to let flavors blend.

Strain vinegar into gift bottles. Store in refrigerator up to 1 month.
Yield: about 3 1/2 cups vinegar

An outdoorsman will enjoy munching strips of savory oven-dried Beef Jerky.

BEEF JERKY

2½ pounds lean round steak
⅓ cup soy sauce
⅓ cup teriyaki sauce
1½ tablespoons liquid barbecue smoke seasoning
½ teaspoon onion powder
½ teaspoon ground black pepper

Place meat in freezer 2 to 3 hours. Trim all visible fat. Cut meat into long, narrow strips, ⅛ to ¼ inch thick.

For marinade, combine remaining ingredients in a small bowl. Place meat slices and marinade in a gallon-size resealable plastic bag or covered nonmetal container. Seal tightly and refrigerate 8 hours or overnight.

Preheat oven to 150 degrees. Remove meat from marinade and drain on paper towels. Leaving space between each strip, place meat on a wire rack over a foil-lined baking sheet. Bake 10 hours with oven door slightly ajar. Meat will lose about half its weight and appear dark brown and dry to the touch when done. Remove from oven and cool completely. Store in an airtight container in refrigerator.
Yield: about 12 ounces beef jerky

SWEET CHRISTMAS PICKLES

2 cups pickling lime
2 gallons cold water
7½ pounds cucumbers, peeled
5 pounds sugar (10 cups)
2 quarts white vinegar (5% acidity)
2 tablespoons pickling spice
Red and green liquid food coloring

In a large nonmetal bowl, combine pickling lime and water; stir until well blended. Slice cucumbers in half lengthwise; scoop out seeds. Cut into ½-inch slices; place in pickling lime mixture. Cover and allow to stand 24 hours.

Using a colander, drain and rinse cucumber slices with cold water

Keep extra jars of Sweet Christmas Pickles on hand for last-minute gift-giving. The zesty slices are great for relish trays or as quick snacks.

3 times. Return slices to large bowl and cover with cold water; soak 3 hours.

Drain again and return to bowl. In another large bowl, combine sugar and vinegar. Place 1 tablespoon pickling spice in each of 2 small cheesecloth squares and tie with string; place in bowl with cucumbers. Pour vinegar mixture over cucumbers;

cover and allow to stand 12 hours.

Divide cucumber mixture in half, placing each half in a separate large Dutch oven with a spice bag; tint red and green. Simmer 50 to 60 minutes or until cucumbers begin to look translucent. Spoon pickles into heat-resistant jars; cover and cool to room temperature. Store in refrigerator.
Yield: about 7 pints pickles

Baking mix provides a head start for making moist, nutty Christmas Bread. The recipe makes enough for four gifts.

CHRISTMAS BREAD

¹/₄ cup butter or margarine, softened
¹/₂ cup granulated sugar
2 eggs
¹/₃ cup applesauce
1 teaspoon vanilla extract
2 cups all-purpose baking mix
1¹/₂ cups chopped candied fruit (we used pineapple and green and red cherries)
¹/₂ cup chopped pecans
²/₃ cup sifted confectioners sugar
1 tablespoon milk

Preheat oven to 350 degrees. In a large bowl, cream butter and granulated sugar until fluffy. Add eggs, applesauce, and vanilla; beat until well blended. Add baking mix; stir just until moistened. Stir in candied fruit and pecans. Spoon batter into 4 greased and floured 3 x 5¹/₂-inch loaf pans. Bake 25 to 30 minutes or until a toothpick inserted in center of bread comes out clean. Cool in pans 5 minutes. Remove from pans and place on a wire rack with waxed paper underneath.

For glaze, combine confectioners sugar and milk in a small bowl; stir until smooth. Drizzle glaze over warm bread. Allow glaze to harden. Store in an airtight container.
Yield: 4 mini loaves bread

CARAMEL PRETZELS AND NUTS

16 cups small pretzel twists
2 cups roasted peanuts
Vegetable cooking spray
2 cups firmly packed brown sugar
¹/₄ cup light corn syrup
¹/₄ cup molasses
1 teaspoon salt
1 teaspoon baking soda
1 teaspoon almond extract

(**Note:** Recipe was tested in a 750-watt microwave.) Place pretzels and peanuts in a 14 x 20-inch oven cooking bag sprayed with cooking spray. In a 2-quart microwave-safe bowl, combine brown sugar, corn syrup, and molasses. Microwave on high power (100%) until mixture boils. Stir and microwave 2 minutes longer. Stir in salt, baking soda, and almond extract. Pour syrup over pretzel mixture; stir and shake until well coated. Leaving top of bag open, microwave 1¹/₂ minutes on high. Stir and shake again. Microwave 1¹/₂ minutes longer. Spread on greased aluminum foil to cool. Store in an airtight container.
Yield: about 21 cups snack mix

Surprise a friend who's prone to snack-attacks with a bag of munchable Caramel Pretzels and Nuts.

ORANGE-CHOCOLATE CHIP SCONES

- 2 cups all-purpose flour
- ¼ cup sugar
- 2 teaspoons baking powder
- 1 teaspoon salt
- ½ cup butter or margarine, cut into pieces
- 2 eggs, lightly beaten
- 3 tablespoons orange juice
- 1 teaspoon vanilla extract
- 1 teaspoon grated orange zest
- ½ cup semisweet chocolate chips
- ½ cup coarsely chopped pecans, toasted
- 1 egg yolk
- 1 teaspoon water
- 1 tablespoon sugar

Preheat oven to 350 degrees. Lightly grease a 9-inch circle in center of a baking sheet.

In a medium bowl, combine flour, ¼ cup sugar, baking powder, and salt. Using a pastry blender or 2 knives, cut butter into flour mixture until mixture resembles coarse meal. Make a well in the center of dry ingredients and add eggs, orange juice, vanilla, and orange zest. Stir just until dry ingredients are moistened. Stir in chocolate chips and pecans.

Pat dough into a 9-inch circle in center of baking sheet. In a small bowl, combine egg yolk and water; brush over dough. Sprinkle with 1 tablespoon sugar. Using a serrated knife, cut dough into 8 wedges, but do not separate. Bake 20 to 25 minutes or until a toothpick inserted in center comes out clean. Cool on wire rack. Serve warm or at room temperature. Store in an airtight container.
Yield: 8 scones

KIWI JAM

- 9 kiwi fruit
- 6 cups sugar
- 1 pouch (3 ounces) liquid fruit pectin
  Green liquid food coloring (optional)

Friends will love these teatime treats! Kiwi Jam is tart and sweet, and Old-fashioned Pears with Ginger can be served with biscuits or pound cake. Orange-Chocolate Chip Scones are simply scrumptious!

Peel kiwi. In a large bowl, crush fruit. In a heavy large saucepan, combine crushed fruit and sugar until well blended. Stirring constantly over high heat, bring mixture to a rolling boil. Stir in liquid pectin. Stirring constantly, bring mixture to a rolling boil again and boil 1 minute. Remove from heat; skim foam. If desired, stir in a few drops of food coloring to intensify color. Spoon jam into heat-resistant jars; cover and cool to room temperature. Store in refrigerator.
Yield: about 6 cups jam

OLD-FASHIONED PEARS WITH GINGER

14 medium pears, peeled, cored, and cut into thin slices
4 cups sugar
   Zest and juice from 1 lemon
1 tablespoon chopped crystallized ginger

In a Dutch oven over medium-low heat, combine pears and sugar. Stirring occasionally, cook until sugar dissolves and forms a thick syrup (about 1 hour). Continue simmering gently until fruit begins to turn translucent, stirring occasionally. Add lemon zest and juice to pears. Stir in ginger and cook 15 minutes. Store in airtight containers in refrigerator.
Yield: about 9 cups pears

ALMOND CREAM LIQUEUR

1 can (14 ounces) sweetened condensed milk
1½ cups whipping cream
1 cup amaretto
⅔ cup vodka
1 teaspoon vanilla extract
2 tablespoons almond extract

Pour sweetened condensed milk, whipping cream, amaretto, vodka, vanilla, and almond extract into a blender and blend until smooth. Store in an airtight container in refrigerator. Shake well before serving. Serve chilled.
Yield: about 5 cups liqueur

Almond Cream Liqueur is easy to make, and it's an elegant holiday gift!

A co-worker will enjoy sipping a mug of Chocolate-Almond Coffee made with this mix. Simply add water for a rich, warming beverage.

CHOCOLATE-ALMOND COFFEE MIX

1 cup non-dairy powdered
    creamer
1 cup sugar
$\frac{1}{2}$ cup instant coffee granules
$\frac{1}{2}$ cup cocoa
1 teaspoon almond extract

Process creamer, sugar, coffee granules, cocoa, and almond extract in a food processor until well blended. Store in an airtight container. Give with serving instructions.
Yield: about 2 cups coffee mix

To serve: Pour 6 ounces hot water over 2 heaping teaspoons coffee mix. Stir until well blended.

BITE-SIZE SNOWBALL MACAROONS

1$\frac{1}{4}$ cups sugar, divided
 $\frac{1}{2}$ cup all-purpose flour
 $\frac{1}{4}$ teaspoon salt
2$\frac{1}{2}$ cups flaked coconut
 4 egg whites
 $\frac{1}{2}$ teaspoon vanilla extract

Preheat oven to 325 degrees. In a medium bowl, combine $\frac{1}{4}$ cup sugar, flour, and salt. Stir in coconut; set aside. In another medium bowl, beat egg whites until soft peaks form; add vanilla. Gradually add remaining 1 cup sugar; continue to beat until mixture is very stiff. Gently fold coconut mixture into egg white mixture. Drop half teaspoonfuls of mixture onto a lightly greased baking sheet. Bake 9 to 11 minutes or until bottoms are lightly browned. Transfer to a wire rack to cool. Store in an airtight container.
Yield: about 10 dozen macaroons

Celebrate the season in style with a gift of melt-in-your-mouth Bite-Size Snowball Macaroons.

You won't believe how easy it is to make irresistible Lemon Sandwich Cookies! They're so delightful that no one can eat just one.

LEMON SANDWICH COOKIES

1½   packages (12 ounces each) butter-flavored crackers
1   can (16 ounces) lemon-flavored ready-to-spread frosting
2   pounds, 10 ounces vanilla candy coating
¼   teaspoon lemon-flavored oil (used in candy making)

Place half of crackers (about 75 crackers) on waxed paper. Spoon frosting into a pastry bag fitted with a large round tip. Pipe about 1 teaspoon frosting onto each cracker. Place remaining crackers on top of frosting and press lightly. In a heavy medium saucepan, melt candy coating and lemon oil over low heat. Remove from heat. Place each cracker sandwich on a fork and dip into candy coating until covered. Place on waxed paper and allow candy coating to harden. Store in an airtight container in a cool place.
Yield: about 6 dozen sandwich cookies

MINT LAYERED BROWNIES

½   cup butter or margarine
2   ounces unsweetened baking chocolate
1   cup sugar
1   teaspoon vanilla extract
2   eggs
¾   cup all-purpose flour
½   teaspoon baking soda
¼   teaspoon salt
1   dozen 1½-inch-diameter chocolate-covered mint candies

Preheat oven to 350 degrees. In a medium saucepan, melt butter and chocolate over low heat. Remove from heat; transfer to a large bowl. Add sugar and vanilla; beat until smooth

All the goodness of a favorite seasonal beverage is stirred into remarkably creamy Eggnog Fudge.

CR...

1 pound vanilla candy coating
¹/₂ cup extra-crunchy peanut butter
1 package (6 ounces) semisweet
   chocolate chips

Place candy coating in a
medium microwave-safe bowl.
Stirring frequently, microwave on high
power (100%) until candy coating
melts. Stir in peanut butter. Spread
peanut butter mixture in a greased
10¹/₂ x 15¹/₂-inch jellyroll pan.
Place chocolate chips in a small
microwave-safe bowl. Stirring
frequently, microwave on high power
(100%) until chocolate melts. Pour
chocolate over peanut butter mixture;
swirl chocolate with a small spatula or
knife. Chill until candy hardens.
Break into pieces. Store in an airtight
container in a cool place.
Yield: about 1¹/₂ pounds candy

*Everyone will agree that this Crunchy Tiger Butter is "grrrreat!" The
confection is quick to make in the microwave.*

A loaf of scrumptious Orange-Pecan Bread makes a wholesome holiday gift.

ORANGE-PECAN BREAD

    3   cups all-purpose flour
  3/4   cup finely chopped pecans
    1   package dry yeast
 1 1/2 teaspoons sugar
 1 1/2 teaspoons salt
    1   teaspoon dried orange peel
    1   cup plus 1 tablespoon milk
  1/4   cup butter or margarine
    1   teaspoon orange extract
        Vegetable cooking spray

In a large bowl, combine flour, pecans, yeast, sugar, salt, and orange peel. In a small saucepan, combine milk and butter. Stirring occasionally, cook over medium-low heat until milk mixture reaches 130 degrees. Remove from heat; stir in orange extract. Add milk mixture to dry ingredients; stir until a soft dough forms. Turn dough onto a lightly floured surface and knead about 5 minutes or until dough becomes smooth and elastic. Place in a large bowl sprayed with cooking spray, turning once to coat top of dough. Cover and let rise in a warm place (80 to 85 degrees) 1 hour or until doubled in size.

Turn dough onto a lightly floured surface and punch down. Place in a greased 5 x 9-inch loaf pan. Spray top of dough with cooking spray, cover, and let rise in a warm place 1 hour or until doubled in size.

Preheat oven to 375 degrees. Bake 30 to 35 minutes or until golden brown. Cool completely on a wire rack. Store in an airtight container.
Yield: 1 loaf bread

Christmas morning breakfast will be unforgettable with pancakes made using Almond Pancake Mix. Whole-wheat flour and ground nuts add hearty texture to the cakes.

ALMOND PANCAKE MIX

    3   cups nonfat dry milk powder
 2 1/2 cups all-purpose flour
    1   cup whole-wheat flour
    1   cup finely ground almonds
  1/3   cup baking powder
  1/3   cup sugar
    2   teaspoons salt

In a large bowl, combine dry milk, flours, almonds, baking powder, sugar, and salt until well blended.

Store in a resealable plastic bag. Give with recipe for pancakes.
Yield: about 7 1/2 cups pancake mix, enough for 3 batches of pancakes

To make pancakes: In a medium bowl, combine 2 1/2 cups pancake mix, 1 1/4 cups water, 1 egg, and 2 tablespoons vegetable oil. Stir just until moistened. Heat a greased griddle over medium heat. For each pancake, pour about 1/4 cup batter onto griddle and cook until top of pancake is full of bubbles and underside is golden brown. Turn with a spatula and cook until remaining side is golden brown. Regrease griddle as necessary. Serve with butter and syrup.
Yield: about 1 dozen 5-inch pancakes

Bursting with red-hot flavor, Cinnamon Candy Sauce will add cheer to any dessert. It's easy to make with only three ingredients!

CINNAMON CANDY SAUCE

- 1½ cups whipping cream
- 1 jar (7 ounces) marshmallow creme
- 1½ cups finely crushed hard cinnamon candies (about fifty 1-inch-diameter candies)

In a medium saucepan, combine whipping cream and marshmallow creme over medium heat. Whisking constantly, add a small amount of crushed candies at a time to cream mixture until candies melt, reducing heat if mixture begins to boil. Serve at room temperature or chilled over cake, baked fruit, or fruit pie. Store in an airtight container in refrigerator.
Yield: about 2½ cups sauce

CHRISTMAS COOKIE KITS

- 1 cup butter or margarine, softened
- ½ cup vegetable shortening
- 5 cups all-purpose flour
- 2½ cups granulated sugar
- 1 cup firmly packed brown sugar
- 2 teaspoons baking powder
- 1 teaspoon salt
  Cookie cutters and red and green decorating sugars to give with mixes

In a small bowl, beat butter and shortening until fluffy. In a large bowl, combine flour, granulated sugar, brown sugar, baking powder, and salt. Using a pastry blender or 2 knives, cut butter mixture into dry ingredients until mixture resembles coarse meal. Divide cookie mix in half and place in 2 resealable plastic bags. Store in refrigerator. Give each mix with a 3-inch star-shaped cookie cutter, decorating sugars, and recipe for Christmas Cookies.
Yield: about 11½ cups cookie mix

CHRISTMAS COOKIES

- 1 bag (about 5¾ cups) Cookie Mix
- 1 egg
- ¼ cup water
- 1 teaspoon vanilla extract

Preheat oven to 375 degrees. In a large bowl, combine cookie mix, egg, water, and vanilla; stir until a soft dough forms. On a lightly floured surface, use a floured rolling pin to roll out dough to ¼-inch thickness. Use cookie cutter to cut out cookies. Transfer to a greased baking sheet. Sprinkle cookies with decorating sugar. Bake 6 to 8 minutes or until bottoms are lightly browned. Transfer cookies to a wire rack to cool. Store in an airtight container.
Yield: about 3½ dozen cookies

A youngster will love creating festive decorated treats with the help of a Christmas Cookie Kit (and some assistance from Mom). Include cookie mix, cookie cutters, baking instructions, and decorating sugar in the kit.

Light, fluffy Cinnamon Puffins are simply irresistible! Bag up a batch of the cinnamon-sugar-coated treats for a favorite teacher.

Perfect for an ice-cream fan, Plum Ice Cream Sauce blends rich fruit flavor with traditional fudge sauce.

CINNAMON PUFFINS

1 1/2 cups all-purpose flour
1 1/2 teaspoons baking powder
  1 teaspoon ground nutmeg, divided
1/2 teaspoon salt
  1 cup sugar, divided
1/3 cup shortening
  1 egg
1/2 teaspoon vanilla extract
1/2 cup milk
1/2 cup butter or margarine
  1 teaspoon ground cinnamon

Preheat oven to 350 degrees. In a medium bowl, combine flour, baking powder, 1/2 teaspoon nutmeg, and salt. In another medium bowl, beat 1/2 cup sugar, shortening, egg, and vanilla until well blended. Add flour mixture to creamed mixture; beat in milk until smooth. Fill each cup of a lightly greased 12-cup muffin pan two-thirds full with batter. Bake 20 minutes or until light golden brown. Melt butter in a small saucepan. In a small bowl, combine remaining 1/2 cup sugar, cinnamon, and remaining 1/2 teaspoon nutmeg. While puffins are warm, dip in butter, then in sugar mixture, coating thoroughly. Store in an airtight container.
Yield: 1 dozen puffins

PLUM ICE CREAM SAUCE

1/4 cup cocoa
1/4 cup hot water
  1 jar (18 ounces) plum jam or preserves
  1 teaspoon vanilla extract
1/2 cup finely chopped walnuts

In a small bowl, stir together cocoa and water until cocoa dissolves. In a small saucepan, melt jam over medium-low heat, stirring occasionally. Add cocoa mixture and vanilla; stir until well blended. Stir in walnuts. Remove from heat. Serve warm or cold over ice cream. Store in an airtight container in refrigerator.
Yield: about 2 1/4 cups sauce

Help a special couple celebrate the holidays with a bottle of spirited Spiced Apple Wine. The mellow beverage is flavored with cinnamon, cloves, and cardamom.

SPICED APPLE WINE

3 medium unpeeled cooking apples, cored and finely chopped (about 4 cups)
1 cup sugar
2 tablespoons water
3 cinnamon sticks, broken into pieces
4 whole cloves
3 cardamom pods, crushed
1 bottle (750 ml) dry white wine

Combine apples, sugar, and water in a large saucepan. Cook over medium-low heat about 3 minutes or until sugar is dissolved. Place spices in a small square of cheesecloth and tie with kitchen string. Add spice bundle and wine to apple mixture; cook 5 minutes longer. Remove from heat and allow to cool. Place in a covered nonmetal container in refrigerator 2 to 4 weeks. Strain wine and pour into gift bottle. Store in refrigerator.
Yield: about 4 cups wine

SUGAR-FREE STRAWBERRY SPREAD

1 envelope unflavored gelatin
1/4 cup white grape juice
3 cups chopped fresh strawberries
2 tablespoons frozen unsweetened cranberry juice concentrate, thawed
2 tablespoons water
1 tablespoon freshly squeezed lemon juice

In a small cup, soften gelatin in grape juice. In a medium saucepan, combine strawberries, cranberry juice concentrate, water, and lemon juice. Stirring occasionally, bring mixture to a boil and simmer, uncovered, 8 minutes. Remove from heat and stir in gelatin mixture until dissolved. Cool to room temperature. Store in an airtight container in refrigerator.
Yield: about 2 cups spread

Naturally sweetened with fruit juices, Sugar-Free Strawberry Spread has a pleasantly tart taste that reflects the true flavor of the berry.

Send warm wishes with a jar of Spicy Salsa. It's easy to make using items from your pantry.

Ring in the season with a batch of chewy Apricot Delights topped with pecan halves. The fruity tidbits make luscious hostess gifts or party treats.

SPICY SALSA

- 1 can (14½ ounces) diced tomatoes
- 1 can (10 ounces) diced tomatoes and green chiles
- 1½ tablespoons dried minced onion
- 1 tablespoon chopped jalapeño peppers
- 1 tablespoon ground cumin
- 2 teaspoons dried cilantro
- 1 teaspoon garlic powder

Combine tomatoes, tomatoes and green chiles, onion, jalapeño peppers, cumin, cilantro, and garlic powder in a heavy medium saucepan over medium-high heat. Cook 7 minutes or until mixture comes to a boil. Remove from heat. Serve at room temperature with tortilla chips. Store in an airtight container in refrigerator.

Yield: about 3 cups salsa

APRICOT DELIGHTS

- ⅔ cup freshly squeezed orange juice
- 1 package (16 ounces) dried apricots
- 2 cups sugar
  Sugar
- 1¾ cups pecan halves

Process orange juice and apricots in a food processor until puréed. Combine apricot mixture and 2 cups sugar in a heavy medium saucepan. Stirring constantly over medium-high heat, bring mixture to a boil. Continuing to stir, reduce heat to medium and boil 12 to 14 minutes. Remove mixture from heat; allow to cool 20 minutes.

Drop teaspoonfuls of apricot mixture into a small bowl of sugar. Press a pecan half into top of each candy; spoon sugar over candy to coat. Sprinkle waxed paper with sugar. Use a fork to carefully transfer candy to waxed paper to cool. Store in single layers between sheets of waxed paper in an airtight container.

Yield: about 7½ dozen pieces candy

Reel in the catch of the day with a bag of tasty Lemon-Dill Snack Mix! A favorite fisherman will love the fun-to-munch fish-shaped crackers and pretzels.

LEMON-DILL SNACK MIX

2 packages (9¹/₂ ounces each)
  fish-shaped Cheddar cheese
  crackers
1 package (5¹/₂ ounces) small
  fish-shaped pretzels
2 cups slivered almonds
³/₄ cup butter or margarine, melted
2 envelopes (1.8 ounces each)
  lemon-dill sauce mix

Preheat oven to 300 degrees.
Combine crackers, pretzels, and
almonds in a medium roasting pan.
In a small bowl, combine melted
butter and sauce mix. Pour over dry
ingredients; toss until well coated.
Bake 30 minutes, stirring every
10 minutes. Allow to cool. Store in
an airtight container.
Yield: about 16 cups snack mix

ANTIPASTO

2¹/₃ cups vegetable oil
 ¹/₃ cup tarragon wine vinegar
 ¹/₃ cup grated Parmesan cheese
  2 tablespoons olive oil
  2 tablespoons lemon juice
  1 tablespoon Italian seasoning
  1 teaspoon salt
 ¹/₂ teaspoon dry mustard
 ¹/₂ teaspoon freshly ground black
    pepper
  1 clove garlic, minced
 ¹/₄ teaspoon paprika
 ¹/₈ teaspoon ground red pepper
  1 can (14 ounces) artichoke
    hearts, drained and halved
 12 whole fresh mushrooms
  1 green pepper, diced
  1 sweet yellow pepper, cut into
    chunks
 ¹/₂ cup pitted whole black olives
  1 jar (4 ounces) diced pimientos,
    drained

For dressing, combine vegetable oil,
vinegar, Parmesan cheese, olive oil,
lemon juice, Italian seasoning, salt, dry
mustard, black pepper, garlic, paprika,
and red pepper in a medium bowl;
stir until well blended. Place artichoke
hearts, mushrooms, green pepper,
yellow pepper, olives, and pimientos in
a 1¹/₂-quart jar with a tight-fitting lid.
Pour dressing over vegetables; shake
to blend. Allow antipasto to marinate in
refrigerator 6 to 8 hours. Transfer to gift
container. Give with recipe for Pasta

Give a taste of Italy with a jar of flavorful Antipasto. The mixture can be served by itself or tossed with cooked pasta.

Salad, if desired.
Yield: about 5¹/₂ cups antipasto

To make Pasta Salad: Toss 2 cups
Antipasto with 1 pound cooked pasta.
Chill before serving, if desired.

INDEX